Praise for *Survive and Advance*

"I've had the honor of working with my man Derek Lewis and witnessing firsthand his unwavering dedication to uplifting HBCUs, student-athletes, and our broader culture. This book is a testament to his passion, his wisdom, and his relentless pursuit of excellence. Derek's impact on our community is immeasurable, and his ability to inspire a new generation to reach for greatness is truly remarkable."

COACH PRIME (DEION SANDERS), NFL Hall of Famer and *New York Times*–bestselling author of *Elevate and Dominate*

"Derek Lewis's *Survive and Advance* is an inspirational and authentic account of how, against all odds, you can use early life challenges to fuel overwhelming success. His raw honesty is captivating, and his steely determination, love of family, entrepreneurial spirit, and desire to make a difference are remarkable. Bravo, Derek, for sharing your bold journey to the top, and for climbing!"

DARRELL K. WILLIAMS, President of Hampton University

"Derek Lewis's journey is nothing short of inspiring, and his unwavering commitment to excellence shines through every page. As someone who has had the privilege of working closely with Derek, I can attest to his incredible vision and leadership. This book is not just a memoir; it's an invaluable resource filled with lessons on resilience, determination, and Black excellence. I wholeheartedly believe it will inspire and empower many."

PINKY COLE HAYES, Founder and CEO of Slutty Vegan

"Derek Lewis is an extraordinarily brilliant mind and equally a reverential leader that served his community throughout his astonishing career. This book chronicles his life journey, which was so aspiring and fascinating that once I started reading it, I could not put it down until I finished. Derek's name truly rings as one of the great innovators and leaders of our community, and this book is a perfect read for a blueprint on how to survive and advance!"

CHARLES MCCLELLAND, Commissioner of the
Southwestern Athletic Conference (SWAC)

"As someone who has not only witnessed but also walked alongside Derek Lewis in both personal and professional realms, I am thrilled to endorse his debut book, *Survive and Advance: Lessons on Living a Life without Compromise*. This book is a road map for living a life of integrity, resilience, and unwavering commitment to one's values. Derek's journey from the challenging streets of Washington, DC, to the heights of corporate America is a testament to what is possible when you refuse to compromise on what truly matters. Whether you're facing personal challenges or striving for professional success, Derek's insights and experiences offer invaluable lessons that can guide you. I truly believe that *Survive and Advance* is a valuable resource for anyone looking to make a meaningful impact without losing sight of their principles."

DERRICK HAYES, Founder and CEO of Big Dave's Cheesesteaks

"Derek Lewis's leadership insights are truly transformative. Drawing from his extensive experience as a long-time executive at PepsiCo, Derek combines a unique blend of empathy and business acumen that sets him apart. His commitment to nurturing and empowering his team, while relentlessly driving for exceptional business results, is a testament to his exceptional leadership qualities. Derek's diverse approach to leadership not only inspires but also delivers tangible success, making him an invaluable voice in the business world."

ALEX MARTINS, CEO of the Orlando Magic

"Advancement and adversity are strange-yet-familiar bedfellows. At times one propels the other, and at other times one prevents the other. Survival is often understood as a state of being no one should stay in for too long, but I offer that for those who came before us, survival was one of the sharpest tools in their leadership kit, and as a result survival manifested as what we can enjoy as *thrival*. My friend Derek Lewis advanced adversity and bequeathed the privilege of surviving in its new form, *thriving*. As I always say, #TakeNotesDoItBetter. The human story presented in this book is now the floor of what is possible for you. Suit up!"

CAROLINE WANGA, President and CEO of Essence Ventures and author of *I'm Highly Percent Sure*

SURVIVE+
ADVANCE

SURVIVE +

**Lessons on
Living a Life
without
Compromise**

ADVANCE

DEREK LEWIS

with **Elle Glencoe**

PAGE TWO

Cataloguing in publication information is
available from Library and Archives Canada.
ISBN 978-1-77458-468-2 (hardcover)
ISBN 978-1-77458-469-9 (ebook)

Page Two
pagetwo.com

Edited by Scott Steedman
Copyedited by Crissy Boylan
Proofread by Alison Strobel
Jacket and interior design by Cameron McKague
Jacket photos by Carey Sheffield
Interior photos courtesy of Derek Lewis,
except where credited otherwise
Printed and bound in Canada by Friesens
Distributed in Canada by Raincoast Books
Distributed in the US and internationally by Macmillan

25 26 27 28 29   6 5 4 3 2

realdereklewis.com

CONTENTS

INTRODUCTION

EARLY 2020 hit us all hard. I know I don't need to remind you about the chaos of the pandemic, the fervor of the global Black Lives Matter protests, and the social and political confusion that had beset the United States for months. But early 2020 hit me hard in a different way, a personal way.

Decades earlier, when he was only twenty years old, my brother Butch lost his life back home in Washington, DC.

I was out of town when Butch was murdered in the streets of DC, and my family couldn't find him. He wasn't taken down by police officers; he wasn't the subject of a racialized attack, but it took five days—long, harrowing days starting on New Year's Eve—before the police knocked on my mom's door to inform her of this tragic news. That was a time that I never forgot but had long since compartmentalized.

The deaths of young Black men in the early days of COVID forced me to remember the details of Butch's life, his last weeks, his too-short existence. Too many Black people were dying, and they were losing their lives without reason or sense. Over the two decades prior to 2020, the Black population in the US had suffered 1.63 million excess deaths and more than 80 million years of potential life lost due to increased mortality risk relative to everyone else, I heard CNN blare.

All my life, I had learned to survive and advance. I chose to superpower my work ethic and commitment so that I would be safe, so that my family would be safe. I demanded a different future for myself from that of my brother, from my father, from some of the kids I played basketball with on neighborhood courts. I understood struggle. My days were a lived experience of constant discomfort and uncertainty that I needed to escape, but I wanted to hold myself high.

I did not want to give in to the fears and violence that had scarred my childhood.

I did not want to die.

As the protests played out on the news, I started to think back to my childhood, the things I'd witnessed, the stories I'd heard around the neighborhood, the ways that we kept ourselves to ourselves. The heightened racial tension of 2020 harkened back to the civil rights era of the 1960s, and it felt like it was only getting worse. I know what it's like living in a community where you don't know what's going to happen next, and where racial and non-racial violence is a given. Every day, you're watching the news and you see someone with a face like yours, with skin like yours, with a family like yours, getting killed. You're angry and you're scared at the same time.

The more the news footage played out on television, the more my revisited trauma wore me down emotionally, mentally, physically.

But the thing is, I wasn't an activist.

When everything went down, I was thinking about the fact that I had great relationships with people in authority, including law enforcement. I had never been the victim or played the victim; I had always just worked harder, faster, smarter, and kept my head up high. While all of this was taking place on the streets, my responsibilities were inside a Pepsi boardroom.

I was living in my own bubble of safety, my wife and kids at my side.

But what if that bubble burst? What would happen to us? Would my kids be safe driving around at night? What the hell was going on?

I had created a pathway for myself, a pathway to survive and advance, and I hoped to God that I could hold the line.

PEPSI IS A GREAT COMPANY. In fact, it's an excellent company. I owe my career to Pepsi, and I will always be a loyal Pepsi consumer. I had worked for Pepsi for over thirty years, working my way up from a just-out-of-college Pepsi sales management trainee to the C-suite, taking on multiple president-level roles, beginning in 2012 as the leader of the Pepsi North America Field Sales Operations Organization. By the time 2019 rolled around after a reorg, my role was President, PepsiCo Beverages North America, South Division.

During the pandemic, the demand for Pepsi's products got stronger and stronger as time went on. With everybody staying at home, Pepsi orders were regular and rampant through large supermarket chains and Amazon deliveries.

Even so, there was an undercurrent of despair in the atmosphere, especially where people of color were concerned. It wasn't just my own family feeling the fear. Small businesses were going bankrupt; unlike the chains, these were the community-based businesses run by minority owners and workers. In the most socioeconomically challenged neighborhoods, it became even more difficult just to get by; people were living check to check, more of them falling below the poverty line every day. There was more downward pressure in these neighborhoods because fear and mandates kept people indoors, and no sales meant no work.

People were going broke. People were going crazy. And people were getting killed.

In my division at Pepsi, we were the pacesetters. Throughout the pandemic, our entire team operated with a strong safety, service, and support mindset every day, focusing on our associates, our customers, and our communities. As a result of our efforts, we led growth performance on revenue, market share, profit, and people. We had already achieved those goals, and more.

There was something at the back of my head, something more that I needed to do. Something that just clicked one day.

"This is not a time for you to just play it safe," I said to myself. "This is not a time for you to be afraid or second-guess yourself. This is a time for you to lead. You've been prepared for this. You've dealt with struggle, trauma. You've dealt with worse. Now's your moment. Don't run from it. Step into it."

I had to respond. I needed to respond for the company's sake, for my own peace of mind, and for the safety of my family. I needed to know that I was doing what I could, as soon as I could, to ease that tension in the community and within myself.

For every one of my nearly thirty-five years at Pepsi, I had made myself untouchable. Because I had already built the reputation I needed to get people to trust me, I was able to cash in all my chips at once. I put everything I had achieved on the table. As the violence escalated in the background of the pandemic, I did what I could within the company, and I did it as fast as I could. I had to make a point of getting myself inserted. I had to lift up my team, peers, and associates throughout the company. I had to create a strategy that addressed everything that was going on outside our company walls.

By 2022, I had become the first President, Multicultural Business and Equity Development at PepsiCo North America.

I led this newly established business unit dedicated to addressing inequalities for historically excluded people and underserved businesses and communities, which we called our Racial Equality Journey. After decades leading sales teams across the continent, and especially as I watched what was happening around us all as the protests wore on, this was a role that had profound meaning for me.

But two years after the pandemic started, I also had a deep sense of having outgrown the very intense operational elements of the business. I could start to feel it, this idea that I had given more than thirty years of my life to this company and that there had to be something more, something else that I wanted to do with my time on this planet.

"SURVIVE AND ADVANCE" is a quote attributed to basketball coach Jim Valvano during his North Carolina State Wolfpack's miracle run to the 1983 NCAA championship. Coach V's team wasn't going to win that championship until he taught them to focus on what was happening in front of them, right then, right now, and nothing else. Survive the pivot. Survive the toss. And then eke your way forward. The idea of survive and advance is one of the reasons I love basketball. There is a lot you can do in a confined space, but games are won and lost over the course of hundreds of points and thousands of strategic moves.

Coach V is correct. We don't have to do everything all at once. We have to get better at the little things before we can get better overall. We have to get into the right mindset to feel like we can win, on the court and at life.

As I was stepping into the fray during the pandemic, I realized that the stakes were getting higher, much higher than when I had first walked in the door at Pepsi. I needed to do something more with the skills I had gained, with the relationships I had built, and with the knowledge that I could deliver real results, even with very few resources. The Racial Equality Journey was great for the company, but there was more to my life than that one project. There were more businesses than Pepsi. There were more communities than my own. There were more leaders than the ones around my boardroom table, and there were more people who could galvanize for change out there. I wanted to find them, connect with them, and look at where I could help.

The problem as I saw it was that our communities had lost their fundamental ability to level up. Instead, they were rounding down.

Sure, we were, and we are, surviving. And by *we*, I mean everyone in the United States and everyone around the world as well. The pandemic showed us that we had the resilience to get things done when we needed to and that we could adapt to worse conditions than we had ever known. But in the process, we'd lost our ability to advance. We all know it. We've lost the ability to see one another's gifts, to be authentic and real, to live by our integrity and our values.

In the business world, we can no longer just put out a nice statement about a social issue or write a check. Because there really is no disconnect between business and life, not anymore, and especially not in communities like the one I grew up in.

People work hard *already*. They are *doing their best* already. And the world is getting more challenging to navigate, not less, for all of us.

As business leaders, there has to be real substance to the work that we do. We can't just be signaling; we have to be accountable. We need to move from being go-getters to go-getters *and* go-givers. We must see ourselves as capable of meeting our own elite expectations, the ones that we set for ourselves. We have a responsibility to explore why the racial equality journey is not over. We must believe in social goals that match financial goals, because without a strong community, we will not be able to make decent profits, let alone build the capacity for the kind of social change that will allow us all to advance. Leveling up means that we have to work together and that we won't settle for the bare minimum any longer.

I believe that we can't just survive: we have to advance. As I saw the smartphone videos, the bodycam footage from George Floyd's death, I also saw the invisible death of my brother. I recognized the path that I did not take. And I thought, "It's time." It is time that we emerge from the past that we created and discover a new future. We must, and we will, lift each other up because we can't keep doing this.

And so I saw that door open, the door that led me away from the safety of Pepsi.

Here we go.

1

CHOCOLATE CITY

I N 1981, when I was fourteen, District of Columbia mayor Marion Barry gave me my first official paying job.

Barry had recognized early on in his career that high youth unemployment during summer months was a fairly accurate predictor of youth crime. In Chocolate City, which is what everyone calls the DC–West Maryland divide, kids didn't have anywhere to go when their parents were at work and schools were closed. His solution, which he implemented the first year he was in office, was to offer every young person a job where they could learn, make some money, and get off the streets. It worked for me.

My job involved filing for the public school district in Brookland, right off the subway line. It was a nice neighborhood known for its numerous Catholic institutions. It was pretty simple work, moving files from boxes to cabinets and getting them in alphabetical order. At the time, the minimum wage was $3.35 an hour, and I would put in four hours a day and make almost fourteen bucks, and that was plenty enough for me to make my daily runs to local mom-and-pop stores to get my usual candy or taco chips. But like many Black kids in DC, working at the Summer Youth Employment Program wasn't my only job, or my first job. Most of what I did was off the books, financially speaking. I cut grass. I washed cars. I cleaned homes. I helped senior citizens load their groceries into their cars. I did what I had to do to keep change in my pocket.

When I wasn't at work, I was at school along with my younger brothers, Damon and Devon. Damon was an introverted kid, the smart one. I did well in school, but Damon did better, and he was and is sensitive in a good way. He can see what's coming a mile away, but he's harder on himself than on others. Devon was nicknamed Butch, and it stuck. Butch's personality in childhood was bigger than he was, and you could always hear him coming. As he was the youngest and smallest of us, both Damon and I looked out for Butch. We all got along. We didn't just love each other; we *liked* each other.

I was a Catholic school kid, but I was never baptized, and we weren't brought up in a religious household. The Catholic school, St. John's, was closer than the public school, which made it easier for me to walk there every morning, and it was easier for me to take care of my brothers while my mother was at work. It was inexpensive. Catholic schools are private but they are subsidized by churches, so, for most of these schools in the 1970s, the fees were minimal. Mom had the foresight to make sure that we got a good education, which was a lot more likely in St. John's smaller classrooms compared to the public school system in those days.

Our low-story brick school didn't totally escape violence, but it was smaller and safer than a public school. All the way up to eighth grade, corporal punishment was still allowed. Brother Frank would lay the wood on people, paddling children with discipline issues at lunchtime in our split classroom. The girls would take it better than the boys. They'd say nothing, while the boys would start crying, unable to sit for the rest of the day.

The first time I was paddled, I was in second grade. I actually don't remember what I had done to be marched into the school administration office that day, but I do remember it stinging quite a bit. The paddle had holes in it that would allow the person on the doling end of the whack more speed and power. The nun who administered the blow was very skilled.

Over the course of my time there, I got paddled fewer than ten times, but once I knew the sting, I had to come up with a way to soften that blow. When I was eleven and knew I would be paddled at lunchtime, I came up with a strategic plan: wearing a couple pairs of thermal underwear under my trousers to cushion the blow. I went in the bathroom to check my gear and tighten my belt at eleven a.m., patting my own rear end to make sure that I was totally ready. I walked up to Brother Frank and was like, "Bring it." For some reason, that day he had an appointment and canceled the paddling. I spent the rest of the day sitting in multiple pairs of thermals, sweating.

Being in Catholic school meant you had to attend mass on a regular basis, as a part of the education process. I ended up spending lots of time in our church throughout the school year, especially during the colder months. Often, I would attend the first mass before school started, at seven in the morning, so I could stay warm. I was always intrigued by the rituals performed at mass. I got really good at following the prayers, the songs, the sign of the cross, even though I wasn't baptized. This is not to say that I wasn't among the faithful; I was. I had an early relationship with God that was honed by my school's rituals and teachings. But because we weren't a religious family, believing felt like it wasn't enough. I hadn't been baptized, so I didn't have the credentials. When it came to mass, for example, I would walk up the aisle to take Communion, but I didn't feel like I deserved to go to Communion because I wasn't really Catholic.

THERE WAS A big age gap between us kids. Damon and Butch were born five and seven years after me, respectively, only a year and a half apart themselves. The reason was that my mother and father had an off-and-on relationship, more off than on.

My mother, Barbara, was a sixteen-year-old candy striper and my father, Roland, was twenty-three when their first pregnancy happened. They gave up my only sister for adoption, a sister I didn't know about until many years later. Mom was eighteen when Roland came back. That resulted in a second baby, me. At that point, they were pushed into getting married on the promise that my maternal grandparents would help them out with the rent on their first apartment, in the Mayfair building in suburban DC.

That marriage certificate and free apartment didn't keep Roland at home with his wife and kids. All I knew was that my parents weren't the same as the other adults I knew, including my grandparents. There were lots of divorced families and single parents out there, but my parents stayed married even though we only saw my father once in a while. When he had money in hand, he'd be gone for weeks or months at a time. Roland would steal anything not glued down; Mom would have to take her checkbook to work so that Roland wouldn't write himself checks from her account. We learned not to be attached to any of our possessions because we never knew when they'd be gone.

When Roland did live with us, he didn't pretend to be a father. He slept on the couch or in my bedroom, even on the floor, not in Mom's bed. Damon and I called him *Roland*, not *Dad*. I don't think Butch really ever knew Roland at all.

More than anything, Roland was confusing. I didn't understand his role in the household. I knew that he was my father, but I never really understood why he was there. I knew that he could tell me what to do, but I didn't see him run the household. That was my mom's role.

Roland's moods changed a lot, and there was no predicting who he would be on any given day. He was charismatic, had the gift of the gab, and could talk anyone into anything. Almost.

What I remember most about Roland was being his lookout.

"PUT A DIME in your sock," Roland said every time he took me out. "We go out at five. If something happens, you need to make a phone call to your mother, come pick you up."

"What are we gonna be doing?"

"It's gonna be a long night. Just remember, you never show your cards. You keep that dime in your sock. Don't pull it out unless you need to call Barbara."

By the time I was seven or eight, Roland would take me out so that I could help him and his friends.

Roland had a system for shoplifting household items like electronics, kitchen appliances, and other miscellaneous wares from department stores.

Regular customers buying a toaster oven, TV, or clock radio would go to one of the service tills where they'd pay for the item, and it would be bagged up, stapled, and sealed with the color tape the store was using that day to identify a purchased item from one that wasn't paid for yet.

The department store bags were always the same. The tape was the key. I don't know where he acquired the tape rolls, but somehow Roland had acquired every color they used, all ready to go. Once we clocked the color of the day, he would put the plan in motion.

I would scoop up the package, place it in the shopping cart, proceed out the exit, and place the item in the trunk of the car. It was that easy. No one ever stopped me or asked questions. I had the right bag and the right tape. I even had the right-looking receipts on hand.

Sometimes I did multiple trips in the same store; sometimes we went to a different store. I can't remember how many times we played out the same scenario, but it was a lot. I didn't know why we were even taking all of those small appliances until I put two and two together: Roland was selling these items for cash to fuel his substance abuse habit. Just before a transaction took place, I was asked to walk away for a few minutes. I would either go get a soda and chips, or quietly sit in the car and listen to the radio until he got back.

I didn't ask any questions.

I just went with the flow.

I followed orders. Who was I, at eight years old, to inquire about what was going on? This was real stuff. The name of the game was survival. That's what Roland was trying to do, and it was what I was trying to do. We were in hustling mode. But it was also the time I got to hang out with my dad, watching him in his element with his friends, talking, laughing. I got to eat at McDonald's for a job well done. It was as good as father-son time was going to be.

I knew what I was doing, and I didn't necessarily like doing it. I did know right from wrong. I was a Catholic schoolboy. I was living in this unique world where, from eight a.m. to three p.m., I was taught all about God and loving each other, respecting people, and the discipline of being a student, and then after school, I was in the streets participating in illegal activities. But more than that, I didn't like what the stuff was doing to my dad.

I also saw the aftermath.

I saw belts and needles and stuff in the closet or on the floor under the bed as Roland's addiction to heroin grew. I didn't like the optics. I also didn't like how his temperament would change depending on whether he was on it or coming off it. I saw his mental health plummet. He was very aggressive with me, and when he snapped, I would catch it. He'd get his cleaning crew; he had to clean my clock. It made no sense, because I did what I was told and I wanted to be cool with my father all the time. I looked up to him, even though he wasn't officially with my mom.

Nothing tracked.

The only thing that made sense was to keep my head down. Roland's hustle eventually caught up with him, and when I was nine, two detectives rang the doorbell and he walked out with them. He walked out without a hassle. They didn't have to put the handcuffs on him.

I remember the times we had to drive up to visit him in prison in Connecticut. I didn't want to see him under those circumstances, but my mom made me go. I didn't understand why we were going through this charade, pretending that we were okay. Again, I knew what was right and what was wrong. I wanted to be smart, know how to step away, so that I could avoid the most extreme compromised positions. Being locked up took away your life. It took away your opportunity. I didn't want to go to jail. I didn't want to die.

CHOCOLATE CITY was a place where Roland Lewis and Marion Barry had to eke their way to survival and where Black men were disenfranchised enough that their economic and social choices were extremely limited.

It's worth noting that Barry was only the second Black mayor in DC since 1874.

In 1867, a few years after Emancipation, Congress granted Black men the right to vote in DC elections, but they took that right away only seven years later because they feared that Black voters would influence political decision-making. This was despite the fact that the Fifteenth Amendment, guaranteeing Black male suffrage, had been passed in 1870.

"What have the people of the District done that they should be excluded from the privileges of the ballot box? ... The old fogies are opposed to negro suffrage; and as they cannot withdraw it, they seek to diminish, if not destroy, the opportunities for its exercise," Frederick Douglass wrote in his newspaper, *New National Era*, in response to the 1874 ruling.

Even as an overwhelmingly Black-majority city, until 1974 DC was run by federally appointed white commissioners. Until then, we didn't have the right to determine how our taxes were spent. How our schools were funded. Where our roads led. What job choices our children had.

We didn't have the right to determine what our future held.

I am not talking about the far-distant past. I am talking about what happened in my own Generation X lifetime.

This is real disenfranchisement that affected, and still affects, real people in the DC area. I'm not saying that my father and my mother didn't have choices, or a community supporting them, or that we didn't make the best of it. But this lived reality affected who we were and what we had to do to make things work, as well as how hard we had to work to shift the status quo over the course of our generation.

It wasn't until Barry, along with other activists, asked Dr. Martin Luther King Jr. to meet with community leaders and lead rallies in support of racial justice and DC Home Rule in 1965 that the tide began to shift. In 1967, President Lyndon Johnson appointed Walter Washington as mayor-commissioner along with a nine-member council, at which time DC became the first US city with a Black chief executive.

Most people remember Barry not as a public service innovator but as the punch line he became for getting caught smoking crack cocaine and going to prison midway through his very long career in office. Eventually, he recovered, regrouped, and came back into the political fold, serving a total of four terms in office. He was by no means perfect, like many of us, but he tried and succeeded in making a difference. Barry's Summer Youth Employment Program, still running to this day, became a national model for youth empowerment and employment. Mayor Muriel E. Bowser, who has served several terms in DC, officially renamed it in Barry's honor in 2015.

I am a product of Chocolate City too.

Like my father, I had to hustle. Unlike Roland, and perhaps because of him, I learned that I couldn't shortcut my way to the future.

After my father was arrested, I knew I needed to come out a better person. I knew that by doing what was expected, and by doing *more* than what was expected, I might be able to get there. I had to focus on hard work and determination. And I had to do my best to be a father to my brothers.

As I shifted from childhood to young adulthood, all I knew was that I wanted to get away. I thought to myself, "One day, if I'm really lucky, when I'm fifty-five, I will be able to make $100,000 and live in a single-family home in the suburbs with my wife and my kids. If I'm really lucky, I'd be far away from DC by then."

That's all I ever wanted.

2

JOANING

BY THE TIME I was twelve, I was my own kind of low-level hustler.

Now, I was a good kid, and a smart one. I had my grandparents, who were good people, looking out for me most of the time. But there was no question that I had to take care of the house and my brothers because my mom worked long days at the Government Printing Office in the Capitol.

One of my family jobs was to do the grocery shopping. I'd go to the local Safeway or Giant Food armed with $100 from my mother's pocketbook to buy two weeks' worth of groceries for the four of us. It was a great experience because I learned how to shop, budget, and plan meals for the family. I would ensure we had the basic meals covered, and then I would load up on treats. On top of that, I tried to keep at least five dollars for myself. Most of the items I purchased were on special or private label. I needed to stretch every dollar until the next paycheck. I liked the bigger brands, but buying private label put more food on the table and more leftover change in my pocket.

I had a strategy though. One that made the deal even sweeter.

Every day before school, I'd take my little pile of savings and go to a local mom-and-pop called Asian American. There, I'd stock up on two bags of Taco Doritos and handfuls of Jolly Ranchers and bubble gum. Then I would break down the large bags of Doritos into more than twenty sandwich-sized plastic bags.

"Oh man, yo, where'd you get the Doritos?"

"At Asian American," I'd say, popping one in my mouth.

"Come on, my parents never buy me these kinds of treats," they'd say, looking at me until I handed some over.

For a price.

I'd sell the bags of Doritos at lunch for twenty-five cents apiece. I sold each piece of candy and gum for a nickel. By the time lunch was over, I was putting over four dollars of profit in my pocket every day. It was more than enough to fuel my pinball habit. After school, I'd head over to a place called Bambinos, which was right up the street. I got so good at pinball I only needed two or three quarters to play for an hour. Getting good meant that I had extra money for comic books and Big Gulps from 7-Eleven after playing pickup basketball. As long as I didn't eat into my profits, the model was working fine.

At school, kids were jealous of the money I was making, but they liked that I was their access point to the treats they coveted. I didn't realize it then, but I was learning how to become an entrepreneur at twelve years old. I had the freedom and trust from my mom, as long as I took care of things at home and school. Grades were good, siblings were being looked after, chores were getting done.

I was fine.

EVEN THOUGH I was raking it in in snack futures, it wasn't quite the same when it came to my overall peace of mind.

The uniform I wore to school was pretty run-of-the-mill: I alternated two pairs of corduroy pants and two shirts with a clip-on tie. Because I only had the two pairs, I had to wear one pair two days of the week and the other on the remaining three. I washed them both every weekend and started the next week out the same way. One day, we were playing football in the parking lot, and as I ran to get the ball, I managed to trip and tear a hole in the right back pocket of my pants.

The kids at my school, like lots of middle schoolers, were brutal.

At Catholic school, you're not just surrounded by locals who know your family. It was a melting pot: white kids coming from the suburbs, other kids that were bussing in from the city. And even though a major part of our education was learning right from wrong, it didn't seem to matter. Everything was game for bullying.

They would pick on me about my parents and my unique family setup. They'd call me out if I did well at school as much as if I did poorly.

And so when I wore those corduroys with the hole in the pocket, I would hear about it.

"You're poor," I'd hear them taunting. "You got no money." "You don't have a better pair of pants." "You always wear the same pair of pants."

They called it joaning.

It's a strange word, and one that was extremely local. The term *joaning* was widely used among blue-collar kids, both Black and white, in Prince George's County, the *Washington Post* reported back in the 1980s. The paper fielded theories that suggested it was connected to the teasing comedy style of then-popular Joan Rivers, but apparently that wasn't the case. Even the experts didn't really know its origins.

"'Jonin' is a quasi-ritualized game of verbal insult, with recognized rules for excelling and status rewards," professor J.L. Dillard of Northwestern State University in Natchitoches, Louisiana, told the newspaper. "There was a theory at one time that it came from [the biblical] Jonah, but there's no basis for that [either]. For the record, I'd have to say that I really don't know where it came from. It may be one of those slang words that has a life of its own."

The joaning I experienced at school did take on a life of its own. It wasn't like I was some soft kid. In taking on the bullies, I would dish it right back out. I'd find a mean thing to say back.

"You snaggletooth," I'd chide. "You bow-legged. Your hair's raggedy. So, you talk about my pants? I'm gonna talk about you. I'm gonna talk about your mom!"

But the problem was that I wasn't dealing with a stacked deck. I had to wear those pants, and my pants kept reminding the other kids that I wasn't all that. They had the trump card, and the trump was on my rear end. Sometimes I thought about wearing the other pair of pants five days a week, but as the family's laundry person, I knew that they'd wear out even more quickly that way.

After a few weeks of dealing with it, I went home and talked to my mom.

"Look, can I get another pair of pants? I'm getting all of this talk at school. I can't deal with it anymore. It's ridiculous."

"I haven't gotten paid yet, Derek. I got a five-year-old and a three-year-old in the house, you know? Times are a little tight."

I just got so mad. After talking to Mom, I did the math, and I knew I would have to put up with these pants for at least another semester or until I fully grew out of them.

"One day I'm gonna buy my own goddamn pair of pants," I thought to myself. "I don't want to worry about the holes anymore."

Sure, I was obsessed, but the joaning went on for months and I will never forget the ridicule. I was walking into this abuse nearly every single day, and I was fretting about my pants every night that I couldn't get the good pair washed in time, meaning that they were dirty enough from muddy touch football games that they'd be criticized as well. Every morning at eight thirty, they'd start drilling on me. Sometimes it even led to fistfights if it got too intense. A little bit of shoving, and then it was worse. I kept on thinking that I had to be mean to defend my reputation.

AS MUCH AS my home life was fractious, so was school. It wasn't as if one was a place I could find solace. I know that a lot of kids who had difficulty at home counted on school to be a safe space, and vice versa. But for me, I felt like neither place was entirely my own. At home, Mom was working too hard, and I was responsible for keeping the house. Roland had gone to jail for a spell. At school, I was working to make my grades and working for extra cash.

It was as if I was living the life of an adult and child at the same time.

Everything was about surviving. I was operating in very difficult conditions, every day. I wasn't at risk of dying, and I was lucky to have a mother and family who loved me, but as I got older and met more people, I learned that my life was much more complicated than the average kid's. I was set up to see what might go wrong, and I was angry and, if I admit the truth, a little scared. I was making the honor roll, but I had to deal with the psychological baggage of my childhood, of watching Roland make his deals, of boosting stuff from department stores. The background noise was too much, and I felt like I had to be the man of the house, the one who protected us from the boogeyman out there, by keeping everything tight. At home and at school, I was always on edge. It was all about survival.

Even so, I was still advancing.

I learned to be quick on my feet and quick-witted. I had to protect my flank and find a way to intellectually hold my ground with the joaning. I had to find people's weaknesses and exploit them to defend myself.

I got really good at it. I got really good at joaning.

One day, I remember bringing a bottle of Clorox to school.

"Hey, Ralph," I said, calling out one of the most relentless guys. "You got yellow teeth. I brought you something to clean them with."

All around me, students started cracking up, pointing at Ralph for a change. I left that Clorox bottle sitting next to me on my desk all day. For one day, I got through class without somebody talking smack about me.

After that, I learned how to predict when and where I'd be the brunt of the joke and started preparing for it proactively.

Where were the holes in their lives?

Where were they weak?

How could I prey on them?

Once I had some ideas in my back pocket and could whip them out if needed, the joaning abated. I got back to studying my lessons and playing my pinball and neighborhood basketball. The confidence I was able to muster from my own resilience, my own ability to pivot when I needed to the most, it worked for me. I decided, consciously, that I was not going to stand for the bullying or the ridicule. If you came after me, you were going to get the same in return, and you were going to get it back harder. You were going to feel the pain.

I don't want to say I became a better person, but I learned how to stand my ground.

Perhaps most of all, by the end of middle school, I learned that I did not have to be embarrassed for being the person I was. I didn't have the money to replace things as quickly as others did, but that didn't say anything about who I was as a person. I didn't have to pretend to be somebody I could never be.

JOANING ISN'T much different from the politics in corporate America.

Everyone has to go into meetings where you know that people aren't going to agree with your ideas. They may even talk insultingly about your ideas.

The only difference is, most of the time in the workplace, unlike on the playground, your colleagues don't do it in front of you. That's the reason why it's actually worse when you're an adult compared to when you're a kid: there's an unkind and tacit backhandedness about insults once you get out of grade school. Everybody talks smack about everybody behind their back. Very few people take the time to unpack why they are upset, either, even though that would be the most productive thing to do with our time at work.

But most of the time, people turn down others' ideas for the very simple reason that they have something different that they want to talk about. They have a yearning to position themselves as that 1 percent better than everyone else in the room. It's not that your ideas are poorly thought-out or won't work or cost too much money. It's that they like their own idea better.

How do you find your way forward if everyone is joaning to get in front?

You have to go into that meeting prepared.

You have to assume that three or four people are against your idea already, either in principle or because their agenda doesn't include you.

You have to know what to say to move the needle on your idea alone.

You have to always be ready for someone to throw a grenade on that idea.

You have to predict what those potential grenades are and how to respond to them ahead of time.

If there are any risks in your plan, people will home in on them right away.

Just like that hole in my pants, they will see it and seize on it and never stop.

So, you need to plug those holes ahead of time. Talk about the risks and how you are going to address them and, if you can, use them to everyone's advantage, before the risks even come up in conversation. Remind them of a manageable risk you took care of two years ago that made the company even more money.

As a middle schooler, I learned that I didn't have to be angry. Everything was fair game. Kids learning how to socialize, even poorly, were learning something about each other and about the world around them.

But I also learned about building my own firepower.

My firepower didn't have to involve destroying the other kids; it was more about détente. It was about testing my limits and seeing where I could find my own level of comfort, so that I did not feel defenseless. It was also about understanding the other kids' weaknesses as well as what got their attention.

Knowing what matters to others changes the whole environment. Knowing what matters to others builds bridges, creates safety, and allows you to feel in control.

Even when you feel like your pants are falling down.

3

HAVEN

OM WAS supposed to go to Howard University, but she couldn't start the September of her freshman year because she was giving birth.

Howard is one of over a hundred historically Black colleges and universities (HBCUs) in the United States. Most of these universities are in the South. The list of HBCUs includes all of the accredited private and public institutions created to support Black postsecondary education before the Civil Rights Act of 1964, the end of segregation. Jim Crow laws meant that we weren't permitted to receive an education unless we supported our own. But even in northern states, strict pre-segregation quotas for Black students meant that there were very few open spots for people like my parents and grandparents, even if their grades were on par with their white peers.

It was a privilege for my mom to get into Howard, still one of the top research universities in the DC area. Even so, my two aunts were the only two out of Mom's four siblings to get degrees, graduating in law and nursing. My mother was left behind to care for me and to eke her way up at the Government Printing Office.

By the time I was in high school, I knew it was important to get into a good college. My grandparents and my aunts and my mom wanted to see me reach a bar higher than the one my father had set. I was doing well at school, so I started to think about my next steps—not only because my family expected me to go, but also because I needed a direct line out. I had to turn my L into a W, and I had to get away from DC to do that. I had to be independent. I couldn't stay at home and study locally, because my living environment, well, it wasn't changing. In fact, it was getting worse.

By the time I was in high school, Roland had been gone for a while. Mom had finally had enough. She knew if he didn't have access to her car, he would have no reason to stay with us. Mom found an old Mercury car key, because all the keys look alike, and switched it out for the one on his keychain. When his key didn't fit, Mom told him that my grandfather changed the locks. He threw an ashtray at Mom while she was holding Butch, but it missed both of them and he got up and left. As soon as he turned the corner, Mom was on the phone to her parents asking them to help come change the apartment locks.

But soon enough, Mom had a new boyfriend. And then another. When the guy I'll call Joe moved in with us, things went from bad to awful. Some of Mom's boyfriends were okay, or they were just *there*. Joe was a former soldier who had been stationed in Vietnam. Seemed like every interaction I had with him was filled with tension or got confrontational, got physical. I didn't understand why my mom had to get involved with Joe. She was still working hard, putting food on the table. He wasn't worth her time, but I think she needed to feel the illusion of family stability, the illusion of having a father for her boys, even if it was a distorted, fun house mirror illusion.

One night when I was sixteen, I was just outside the house after playing basketball, and as I opened the door, I could hear my mom trying to calm Joe down.

"Everything's okay. Everything's gonna be alright," she said.

"What's going on?" I said quietly, there on the front step.

"Did you disrespect me? Did you disrespect me?" Joe said, turning on his heel to point at me. "You didn't clean the dishes before you went out, Derek. You're disrespecting me, and you're disrespecting your mom."

"I'm gonna do it tomorrow."

I knew I was talking back. We got into a lot of heated debates, Joe and I, because I was fed up with how he talked to me, to Mom. I knew he cheated on her, and he turned it around and blamed her for his pain. He didn't seem to give a shit about any of us, except to try to get us to do what he wanted, when he wanted. It was just a lot of yelling, a lot of arguing for no reason I could understand. It was weird though. Our family had been a well-oiled machine before he came along, and all he contributed was a couple years of hell.

"You're gonna do it today. Why? Because I'm telling you to."

I could feel myself getting worried about Damon and Butch, watching from the sidelines. I could see them out of the corner of my eye. Damon, always a calm kid, looked quieter than usual. In his mind, he must have been assessing the situation. Butch, the boisterous one, was unusually silent. Damon grabbed Butch and pulled him into the other room, looking back over his shoulder at me as he closed the door.

"No," I said, bringing myself up to my full height as I stepped over the threshold. "I'm not doing something just because you're telling me to. Why would I have to do that?"

It wasn't until he pushed me up against the door I had just opened, hand around my neck, that I saw the Rambo-sized knife in Joe's hand.

In a split second, I knew that things weren't going right. I didn't understand what was happening. In my head, I was thinking this was just too crazy. I was the good kid, the oldest. I took care of my brothers. I took care of the house. Even then, I was still the guy doing the laundry and washing the clothes. And now I was the bad guy? *I* was the one fucking things up? Nothing made sense, and I didn't want to move. I stopped talking. My eyes started to sting. I was genuinely scared for all of us.

"What's wrong, Joe?" I heard my mother's soothing voice behind him. "You're respected, you know? We value you so much." She was playing the game. "I understand how you feel, Joe. We're going to close the door. We're gonna figure this thing out."

Mom was smart. She shot me a look that told me I had to give her some time, let her do things her way for a moment. She knew that she needed to get us out of this mess delicately.

"Derek, you take the boys out for a walk."

"Mom..."

"Joe and I are gonna figure this thing out. You go now. Be back in half an hour."

I didn't know what happened behind the door I closed behind us. I still had my basketball in my hand. I was worried for Mom. I was worried for all of us. I don't know if Joe'd been physically abusing her as well, but my bruises and that knife were enough to make me concerned that I'd be walking into a bloodbath when we got back.

Magically, everything was quiet that night on our return, and I didn't see Joe until the morning when I was washing the dishes.

"I'm leaving to look for a . . . a different opportunity. It just didn't work out with your mom," he said, holding his head high.

It was a very respectful departure, one that I never imagined could happen. I thought it was going to end very, very badly. And it very much might have.

Mom knew. She knew. Some years later, right after I got out of college, I saw Joe's face on the news. He had ended up marrying another woman and becoming a father to her child. Then he snapped and killed his wife, stabbing her multiple times in front of their daughter. He, like Roland, ended up in prison. Somewhere down the line Joe fell off his path, even though Mom helped him that night, helped me, helped our family survive.

I had to break away from everybody and everything.

IN HIGH SCHOOL, the picture I had of my future was very small. With an education, I thought, I could be a government worker like my mom, but the kind with a better salary and benefits. I was thinking I could do a little bit better than my mom. A little bit better than my grandfather. A little better, so that things wouldn't be quite so exhausting, so overwhelming.

But just before my senior year, just before Joe left, something changed in the way that I saw myself in the world.

My mom helped me apply for a summer job at Forest Haven in Laurel, Maryland. It was a state residential school and hospital operated since 1925 by the District of Columbia for children and adults with intellectual disabilities.

I didn't really know much about the place or what kind of job I'd be doing, but I knew that a bus that would pick me up on 8th and H Streets every day at seven thirty in the morning and drop me off at four thirty.

I was excited about the job because that schedule left me plenty of time to get on the basketball court after I got home.

I didn't have the time or the resources to play on the club or recreational basketball teams, even though I was pretty good when it came to getting points on the playground. Every day, a few of us would walk to neighborhood courts to find competitive pickup games that would last until dark. Sometimes we played until midnight if the court had lights. Basketball calmed my mind; it gave me ease after a long day. It was where I felt myself.

When I arrived at Haven the first day, I learned that the staff nickname for the place was the Children's Center. It wasn't nice. Because the residents' development capacity was equal to someone five, six, seven years old, the name stuck.

I was one of four student interns at Haven, but I was the only one assigned to operations. The other three students worked in the administration building pushing paper or behind the scenes in the canteen.

My job was to assist the nurses. That first day, I watched them feeding the residents, bathing them, cuddling and comforting and talking to them. Our role was to make sense of what the residents needed. We had to perceive these needs by listening to what the residents said, which wasn't always clear. The first few days I was there, they didn't talk to me at all. They didn't give me any attention because they didn't know who I was. I had to learn their varied ways of communicating. I had to show up. I had to remember people's names in order to get them to trust me.

Martin, a resident, was a heavy smoker who wore a scrunched-up expression on his face, laughing at me, laughing at himself. We became friends because he was one of the first people I talked to at Haven, and he sort of taught me the ropes. I learned what he liked to watch on TV, the games he liked to play. I realized that when I started figuring all that out,

I put a smile on his face. It was within my power to make him happier, to make others happier, just by paying attention to the small things.

I did harder things at Haven too. Like the rest of the team, I had to clean up pans of urine and feces. I had to serve meals to people who did not have the means to feed themselves. I worked my ass off while I was there. When people needed me to do stuff—the nurses, the doctors, the staff—I did it. I cleaned that place before I left every day. Every day, I asked, "Do you need me to do anything else before I leave?" I took pride in that work.

And I watched the staff at Haven do that job day in and day out, knowing that they stayed longer and worked harder than me. I was only there for the summer; everyone else was there for life. By the end of the first month, I would springboard out of bed to get to work because it mattered to me that I was part of that team, part of that community.

Despite my positive experience at Forest Haven, it's important to note that around eight or so years after I worked there, Forest Haven underwent a forced closure on October 14, 1991, by order of a federal judge. Former residents and their families had come forward about their experiences there, which included physical and sexual abuse, medical incompetence, and deaths connected to improper feeding procedures; the majority of the cases noted by the Justice Department took place in or after the late 1980s, years after I had left the job. While I noticed the limitations on staff time and resources connected to Forest Haven's defunding and deinstitutionalization, I did not witness any resident abuse.

Despite—and in addition to—the crisis that took place at Forest Haven after I left the facility, I witnessed incredible vulnerability there, vulnerability that put my own lived experiences into perspective. The residents and the staff there were vulnerable. I was lucky to have Mom. I was lucky to have my brothers. I was luckier to have my health, physical and mental, and my ability to adapt to what the world threw at me every day. I was lucky to have the wits to get myself into college, to get myself up in the morning, to be organized and focused.

I was lucky enough to know what I wanted to do next.

WORKING AT Forest Haven taught me this amazing thing about the importance of offering care.

Taking care of people, even people we don't know.

Being responsible when friends are vulnerable.

Knowing that when folks don't have everything they need, you may have something to share.

Caring matters the most to people who are in crisis, to people who don't know where to turn. But it also matters in normal situations. Keeping our humanity in mind is just as critical when we're out buying groceries as when we're selling products. Everyone is going through something. No one at Haven knew what I was going through at home, what Joe was putting us through. No one knew that I was scared that one day we'd all end up dead. But when I could turn that pain into taking care of the residents at Haven, I knew there was something good happening. Something small, but wonderful.

Taking care of people mattered at the end of my last summer as a student in DC as well. The internship program's end-of-year celebration invited hundreds of students to come together to recognize our collective accomplishments.

I'll never forget that day. When I heard my name called out from the podium, it didn't compute. The nurses and staff there had nominated me for a special award. I had not known ahead of time that my work at Haven had made such a difference, or that I had been seen. I wasn't honored just for my attendance and program participation; I was singled out for how much I cared.

I savored every moment of that singular feeling of accomplishment. It's something that's stayed with me throughout my career. In high school, I loved basketball, but I learned I loved people even more. I learned emotional awareness from my mother. I learned compassion at Haven. But more than that, I learned that intense feeling of intrinsic reward from doing something that mattered personally to others. I recognized that I was allowed to feel like a good human being because I cared for people.

In that same moment, somewhere inside me, I felt a sense of relief, a reminder of self-forgiveness, an excitement about taking pride in the happiness of others, the feeding of others' needs. I recognized that, maybe, my life was going to work out differently than Roland's, than Joe's, than my mom's. I realized that I could be a good human being by working hard. Everything else, every fear, every sense of self-doubt, it was all in my mind. I had the ability to see myself into a different future than the one that I had expected. Knowing that, trusting that in myself, shifted and validated my life, my choices, from that moment on.

We all have everyday moments where we have choices to make. We notice these moments all the time when we're up against it, when we're faced with frustration behind the wheel, when our children or partner or parents remind us of our flaws, when we listen to our work colleagues take a tone with us. In those moments, we have to decide whether we lean in to old fears or whether we can summon our better selves, our caring selves. The Us that feels elated at making someone's day.

Each of us has the ability to make someone else's life better. And if *you know* that you have the ability to make someone else's life better, then you need to *go do that*.

4

THE REAL 007

ALL I COULD HEAR was my own name.

The noise was deafening. Through the roar of the crowd, I knew I heard it, my name. The crowd was shouting for me. They were shouting and cheering on the sixteen of us in the line. We were now officially part of the Scroller Club of the Beta Chi chapter of Kappa Alpha Psi, Incorporated, also known as the Nupes.

"Derek!"

"007!"

I couldn't see what was going on around me. I was locked in a straight line with my Scroller Brothers, keeping my eye on each next move, each Brother next to me. We had lined up tallest to shortest in our chapter, the exact opposite of other fraternities, at our coming-out party on the Hampton University yard on a cold Sunday evening in January of 1986. Marching to a beat we called "Rough & Tough," we were dressed in black suits with black ties, black shoes, black

Kangol hats, and long trench coats. Our heads and faces were completely shaven.

We were moving in complete unison with every step and every word.

Each of the Nupe pledges was colloquially known as a Scroller, and each Scroller was assigned a line nickname or two. Our line names were chosen to match up with our personality, interests, or image. During the first interest meeting when we had to introduce ourselves, we had to tell the Brothers what we aspired to do once we graduated.

"I kind of want to be an international spy," I said.

They all laughed pretty hard.

"You're joking," they chuckled.

"Nope," I said in all seriousness. I had been thinking about it for a while. I thought I had what it took: I was smart, agile, thoughtful, and it sounded as exciting a career as I possibly could pursue.

"Well, I guess we got a real James Bond mofo here then," someone said, changing the tone of the conversation pretty quickly. And so Bond, 007, became my nickname. I was as surprised as anyone when the name stuck.

The other line name I acquired was The Beast. I had an aggressive temperament while I was pledging. I liked 007 better. In the beautiful arrogance of my youth, I'd decided who I wanted to be, and I tried to rise to the occasion. I was number four on the list of Scrollers.

"Come on, show the intensity, show the grind, show the enthusiasm!" I heard the senior Brothers calling us out as we marched. The crowd loved us. We were in our element. Stepping in line on the yard felt like becoming a Hollywood star, walking down the red carpet for the first time. The crowds, the cheering, the support, the emotion, everything was the highest of highs. We were proud and bold.

We needed to hear those cheers to help deal with the challenge of pledging.

Pledging and being inducted into Kappa Alpha Psi, one of the HBCU fraternities known as the Divine Nine, was one of the most amazing processes that I have ever been through in my entire life. To campus life, this was everything. When new lines came out, it brought a kind of energy I had never seen or experienced before. You were on display now, all day and everyday throughout your official pledging window. If you were chosen to be on line, it was a very big deal, and how you were going to be viewed on campus would begin to change dramatically. The name of the organization was changed in 1915, unique among National Pan-Hellenic Council–affiliated organizations in that it has two names: Kappa Alpha Psi (ΚΑΨ) and Phi Nu Pi (ΦΝΠ). This second name is the source of the nickname for members, "Nupes." Every year, the new Kappa line would take on a Swahili name as well. The year before us, Ngoja. In 1986, we named our line Amerika: a new world, a new order, a new beginning.

We were stepping and marching with pride. Stepping, a percussive song and dance ritual performed by Black fraternities and sororities, makes the body an instrument. We stepped, stomped, clapped, and used the spoken word to express love and pride for our community. We took up space. We were the draw, the big men on campus for that moment. We knew we were noticed. We stayed in line, our line, our day.

I savored every moment.

The evening had started at the foot of the Emancipation Oak. In 1863, the Virginia Peninsula's Black community gathered at this tree in Hampton, Virginia, to hear the first reading of President Abraham Lincoln's Emancipation Proclamation outside the Capitol.

There, the past met the present.

At the entrance of the Hampton University campus, this Virginia oak has lived more than two hundred years, and probably more. The oak wasn't just a gathering place for emancipation, as much as that matters. It was a symbol of freedom ten times over. Southern trees, as Billie Holiday suggested, aren't like those in other forests, and strong oak tree hardwood was by far the preferred species for the 3,446 lynchings of Black men accused of crimes in the South. The most recent of these mob-decision hangings took place in 1968 in Mississippi, one year after my birth. But the oak at Hampton had always been a tree of a different kind, one that supported and created knowledge. During the Civil War, Union general Benjamin F. Butler not only allowed nearby Fort Monroe to become a refuge for those escaping slavery but defined those fearless escapees as contraband of war. Mary Peake, a free woman of color from the North, offered an education to escapees under that tree, something previously forbidden by Virginia law. Beginning on September 17, 1861, fifty students or more would sit with Mrs. Peake under the tree during the day and twenty at night to learn reading, writing, history, and mathematics. Seven years later, Hampton Normal and Agricultural Institute was founded there in that place of sanctuary and freedom, a postsecondary institution that eventually became my beloved Hampton University.

The Emancipation Oak was only the beginning.

I wasn't there alone. At the beginning of 1986, my new Kappa Alpha Psi fraternity Scroller Brothers were there beside me, praying with me, listening to me swear my oath to our brotherhood and the values we represented before taking our first steps into the crowd, hearing the roar of our peers, our beautiful community.

WHEN I PLEDGED KAPPA, all of a sudden I had a new identity.

I came to college knowing that I had one opportunity to become the man I wanted to be, and the clarity of being a Kappa allowed the floodgates to open. In high school, I had no idea what a fraternity was, but it became a big part of my life.

Like most freshman college students back then and even now, I wasn't ready for any of it despite my ability to buy groceries and clean up after myself. Hampton's campus wasn't that big, but instead of being in a tiny Catholic school of a couple hundred students with my mom and grandparents around the corner, I was 180 miles away, living on leafy Chesapeake Bay with five thousand or more people my age. After keeping my head down and my grades high, I had gotten into Hampton just as I'd planned. College life was fine. It was good. It was all part of my plan to create that different future for myself, the one where I didn't have to stay in DC.

In the spring of my freshman year, it was a complete takeover. The fraternities and sororities were at their richest and most vibrant, their new line members stepping in their bright paraphernalia, glowing, excited, showcasing future inductees. They were the ones running the yard, showing up and turning out. They were the somebodies. I saw how the campus gravitated toward them and how we just stopped whatever we were doing to watch Greek pledges pass us by. They were student government leaders, presidents of clubs and extracurricular activities, top achievers across the board. They ran the campus, and by that, I mean that their numbers didn't just include students. The administrators, the deans of the schools, the president of the school, the career counselor, they were all in the Greek system, past and present. I knew they were fraternity and sorority members, but why they were so important to our university, our culture, was a mystery. Why were they holding court on campus? I saw them wearing their three-lettered shirts walking around like they owned the place, and at the time I was thinking, "Who gave these guys the right?"

At the time, I wasn't a joiner. I was the go-to guy, the smooth DC tough guy. At Hampton, I quickly learned that popularity and respect wasn't just granted because of where you came from. You had to go earn it. It was very much a family-like environment on campus where trust and relationship building meant everything. You had to make a real effort both in the classroom and on the block. I didn't know what I was capable of doing, especially in my first year; I was just trying to get decent grades and enjoy the social scene as much as possible. I found my crowd, but I still felt that chronic instability of the unknown.

These Greek organizations had the juice though. And so I started asking questions. I found out about their great contributions to the university, to the community, to the national organizations to which they belonged. And so I allowed my mind to be changed. I allowed for the idea that joining might be a benefit to me, and to the fraternity I chose in return.

All Divine Nine fraternities and sororities have an introduction process to their organizations. Some call it a "Rush" or a "Tea"; others call these gatherings "Info Sessions." We called them "Smokers." A Smoker is basically an interest meeting where the Brothers will talk about Kappa and the chapter and what it means to join up. You had to be a known entity before going to a Smoker, as I learned. This was a heavily intensive social process that began a semester before we were permitted to pledge. The Nupes were scoping out possible line members well before we ever met.

Ngoja had been through a lot in the previous year. In 1984, there was no line and therefore no new Nupes inducted due to internal reasons, and so those Brothers who had planned to pledge had to wait until 1985. Because of that hardship, the process of becoming a Kappa was very, very difficult for those of us who pledged the fraternity in 1986.

Pledging was a lightning-fast immersion into a new cultural world; only a select and grateful few were invited. The process, with its buttoned-up military precision and discipline, was about committing wholly to supporting Kappa. You have to be ready for everything the organization throws at you—physically, intellectually, and mentally. Routines are akin to being in a marching band: the chanting, the singing, lining up in the cafeteria, pivoting, walking together to hold our lunch trays, and following the one-two-three-sit command to eat.

After classes, we'd meet up at the "hole," one of the Scroller's dorm rooms that we turned into a community room during the pledging process. We would march to the café to eat dinner from five to six, then perform on the block for thirty minutes for the crowds. Finally, we'd have study time at the library until eight. After that, we'd march back over to the dorm to change and get prepared for late night activities. Some nights we'd entertain visiting Brothers from other campuses who came to check us out. Each weekday we repeated the same process over and over.

Weekends felt relentless; it felt like we never got a break or time on our own. On the weekends, we volunteered for local community-based organizations like Boys & Girls Clubs and Habitat for Humanity, building houses, serving meals in homeless shelters, spending time with kids, donating backpacks, collecting cans for food drives. I was lucky that I played on the Kappa intramural basketball team, which gave me a few hours to blow off some steam with a couple other talented Scrollers before we had to get back to the grind.

I know, in writing all of this, it may seem that I am overly praising my Kappa experience, but it provided me with a fundamental shift in my identity that I needed to survive. It reinforced to me that I belonged somewhere.

I learned what was important to me, my value structure, and that nothing was impossible.

I did not take shortcuts.

I went through it all, and it was hard. I had moments when I was isolated because of who I was, where I had come from, but I would not give up. I embraced the networking, I embraced the events, I embraced being known in public. Before Hampton, my role models presented me with either day-job drudgery or addiction-fueled nightmares. Being a Kappa absolutely rocket-fueled me to a high-caliber position on campus, one that allowed me to dream differently.

That experience opened me up in a way that I hadn't known was possible. I did not write this poem called "Pursuing the Dream," but it was one of my favorite reflection texts throughout the process.

We all have something that we really desire,
One thing that stands out in our minds.
I have something that I want so, so bad:
To make Kappa Alpha Psi's next line.
This is a dream that's not out of reach
And it all depends upon me.
Nupes are distinguished, smart, and know
where they're going,
And that's how I'm going to be.
They're instilling in me a sense of altruism,
The unselfish concern for others.
This is why I not only want it for me,

But also for my potential brothers.
I've learned the meaning of taking slack,
Helping my brother who's down.
It comes without hesitation because I know
The favor will come back around.
I'm striving for excellence, trying to reach the tops
Of mountains that weren't there before,
I've learned so much to help better myself
And I've yet to learn much more.
We know it's not easy, it's going to be hard
To wear the Krimson & Kreme,
But I know we'll all be there when the smoke clears
Cause we're all pursuing the dream of KAPPA ALPHA PSI.

KEVIN HEATH, a junior from my own stomping grounds of
DC, was the assistant dean of pledges (ADP) in my Scroller
year. That meant that he was our mentor, helping us learn,
listening when we were stressed or worried we wouldn't make
it to the line. There were many who didn't; people peeled off
one by one when they recognized what they were up for, the
work it took, the time. It wasn't easy to balance schoolwork
and getting to know the Kappas, especially as a sophomore
when our professors weren't taking it easy on us anymore.
Kevin and Darin, our second ADP, made sure that all of us, all
of the potentials, were staying close to one another.

During pledging and afterward, I probably spent the most
time with Marc, who is still a great friend to this day. We
were in the same dorm freshman year, and he was a communications major from the Philly area, so we were naturally drawn
to each other. Marc and I hung out a lot with Darryl from
New Jersey, and we knew we were going to go far together.
But every one of my line brothers was someone special.

I remember Trent, a good man early in life who carried himself like our pastor, very disciplined and kind. Darren had leadership potential right from the start and later became our Polemarch, the head of our chapter. Joe, who passed away in 2008, was the most talented and charismatic line brother I had. He could do it all, and he did it all for Kappa. Every man I met showed me something I wanted to emulate. Herm, Laurence, Richard E., Jerry, James, Mark, Dale, Richard F., Bill, and Darryl J. completed the Amerika line. These men are my brothers for life.

I finally had backup.

Suddenly, I realized I had Brothers my age. The word *Brother* came up a lot in our late night pledge talks. My own blood brothers were so many years younger than me, so we had never really been peers. Even though I got along well with Damon and Butch, as I got older, I was always taking care of things, acting as a father figure. I felt that responsibility hang so heavy on my shoulders that I didn't know what it was like to be a real brother, an equal, someone who got to lean on family members. I didn't know what it meant to really want something for myself, something for me alone. Not until I got to Hampton.

When we finally crossed over and officially became Kappas, it was Kevin who gave me a big hug.

"You did it, man," he smiled.

"This was awesome. Awesome. I can't believe we did it," I said, shaking his hand. "Off the charts."

"You're gonna be me next year," Kevin said.

"What do you mean?"

I was trying to hear him, trying to understand what Kevin was saying. It was loud, the campus filled with cheers and music. Behind him, I could see all of the Greek organizations running around with their colors, everyone making noise.

"You're coming into a new chapter. You got junior brothers ahead of you, and you got senior brothers who are graduating," Kevin said. "So you're coming back next year a junior, right, and you're evolving."

"I just got here, Kevin. I'm just... I mean, I want it, but..."

"You're better than you think you are. Derek, I'm going to tell you something you're not going to understand right now. You're not just a kid from DC. You're a strategist, and you care about people. I can see the man you're going to be. And it doesn't hurt that the seniors above us who have rank, they like you. You can do this."

"Okay," I said, hesitant.

"Yes? Okay."

"I can do this?"

"You can do this."

I wanted to serve as a part of Kevin's team. I trusted him, and I trusted Kappa because our traditions at Hampton were part history, part future. In some ways, Kevin was the first man I truly looked up to in life. Roland and Joe weren't stable. My grandfather was older, his life less relatable. Our dean of pledges (DP), Buttons, was also a great leader and mentor, but Kevin was all about us. I absorbed everything he said. He understood where I came from. He knew what was at stake. He got it.

Kappa had that focus, that drive that mirrored my own. I had no problem getting up early and staying up late to make the impact I wanted to make, and my Brothers had the same internalized need to reach beyond their current limitations. For members of Greek organizations across American campuses, knowing that you are a part of an honored and respected history feels good. It feels like connection and community. But what is different about Kappa and all of the Divine Nine is that they bring a very specific and rich history of Black excellence to the forefront of what they do. Achievement is a big part of the fraternity and sorority mentality on American campuses, but Kappa is also about our specific culture. We learned to step because, after the 1739 Stono Rebellion in South Carolina, stepping and drumming had been outlawed; eighty Africans had rebelled against their capture, marching to gather strength in numbers. The Divine Nine reclaimed these cultural acts because they are our birthright. Stepping songs are still housed in each fraternity's and sorority's archives because they belong to us. At the same time, we lived in the present, where, especially in the 1980s, white fraternities represented power within the business world. Our culture met current events and business developments, head-on. Fraternities and sororities at Hampton were not about fighting the power; they were about owning our collective strengths.

Personally, I needed to feel that sense of strength.

When I got to Hampton, I was only just past the threshold of becoming my own person, just beginning to know what I wanted out of my life. Of course, that could be said about just about any other young adult, but given my upbringing I could have gone in any direction, including straight down. The fact that I believed that I could level up and that I could achieve that goal with my integrity intact was fully connected with finding a culture I could believe in. It was connected to finding people to share my journey up and out of my past, people who had also traveled the same path, who just got me without my having to explain.

Like Hampton itself, we Brothers were representing the best of what our shared history had achieved, and we were presenting the possibility for a future bound to knowledge, self-respect, and confidence. We were building the kind of trust in ourselves and in each other that would last a lifetime.

We knew that people were watching, and we weren't going to hide.

TRADITIONS ARE a big part of culture, whether that culture exists in a family, a language, a community, a college, a company, or on the Kappa line. The most game-changing part of Kappa's culture was our commitment to doing the right thing. We had a mission.

Good Brothers.

Good cause.

Good purpose.

The process of building a culture that works is about building a culture where it is possible to win.

As a Kappa, I recognized that there's a physical component to becoming part of a new culture, a new social echelon, that riveting feeling through your body when you know you are changing for the better. There's an emotional component when you recognize your own strengths in getting there. There's a mental component in understanding that you have made the right sacrifices and choices. Very few people demonstrate that they have all three at that right moment when they are ready to be accepted, and when others are ready to accept them in turn. That moment when you hear the knock at your door, you have to be ready to open it.

At the same time, there are many cultural touchstones in the United States that contradict one another. Values of achievement that contradict values of community. Values of social superiority that socially isolate the poor and indigent. But the cultural touchstones that prevail over the long term are not those grounded in hate, in self-loathing, or in fear. The ones that survive—and perhaps this is why businesses survive, why the American dream survives—are grounded in our personal and collective potential.

In work and in life, most people want to achieve. Most people want to be excellent. But you have to have a leadership orientation and a cultural mindset that allows you to win. It's one thing to demand performance or set expectations, but to create a culture where people believe they are capable of feeling good every day, that's harder.

History and tradition both benefit us and get in the way.

At Hampton, we recognized and valued our history, and we put traditions into practice. But we also didn't let that history hold us back. What happened within my Kappa cultural experience was that I faced my past, wholly and fully. I had my Brothers by my side as I looked critically at where I had come from as an individual. I looked at how my experience, and my family's experience, had been shaped by history. But then, almost right away, I was empowered, educated, and elevated by the people I trusted.

We can get so focused on doing things the way we've done things in the past, the way things have worked for so many years. But we also need to be modern; we need to be new thinkers. We need to push ourselves to be better and greater than we were in the past.

In a workplace or in a family home, the same tenets apply. They apply no matter what your personal background.

If you empower your children to make decisions with confidence, they will trust themselves.

If you educate your team on the keys to success in business and listen in return, they will follow your lead.

If you elevate those who stand behind shared values and a shared purpose, you'll create cultural teachers who will pass that message on. If you elevate those who are dependable behind the scenes, you'll create a culture that will stand the test of time. If you elevate those who elevate others, you will build lasting trust.

5

MINUS ONE

THOUGHT WE had it all figured out—until we didn't.

Junior year was supposed to be stellar. Everything was lined up. Just like Kevin said, I was elected as an ADP, and early in September 1986, we organized the pledging process. Together with the other ADP, Mark, we were looking at who would be part of the next line for spring 1987. We completed all of the prescreening, talked to and vetted interested guys, completed our visitation interviews, the works.

And then all of a sudden it was over.

At the end of my own pledging process the previous spring, there had been an incident during our Hell Week, the last hurdle we had to pass before becoming Kappas. The incident had primarily involved visiting Brothers from another campus, but it really affected one member of our line.

Little did I know that the incident got reported up to the regional office and then Kappa HQ. It was serious enough that the university administrators sent us an official notice in January 1987 that we would not be having a line that year. Visiting Brothers or not, it was our responsibility to shoulder. It was only one month before we planned to reveal the new members of our Scroller Club. We had already voted internally on the candidates and were extremely excited to announce their induction, but in a repeat of what had had happened three years previously, our fraternity lost the right to have that line. The university's administrators weren't taking any chances, especially after two unrelated fraternity deaths in the non-Black college community had already made headlines that year on other campuses.

Kevin was devastated. It was his senior year, his DP line, and he had had nothing to do with the ruckus that had led to this decision. Kevin was all about the fraternity. All in as a leader, in service to his community, and to our brotherhood. All of his time was committed to that line, and suddenly it was gone.

We tried everything. We appealed. We called our alumni Brothers to speak on our behalf, but they said we had to wade through it on our own. Nothing worked. It was only a one-line penalty, and we would hopefully be reinstated the following year, but it felt rough after all of the effort we'd put in. We knew we had an excellent line coming in. We tried to keep our heads high. Of course, we still had our Brothers to lean on, but we were a bunch of dejected guys watching all the other Greek organizations' lines go by.

We felt like outcasts, and my role as ADP was pretty much moot. And it was worse than that. There were altercations between Brothers. We got into arguments because everybody was pissed off about what had happened, and we took it out on each other.

Over the summer of 1987, Kevin and I would talk often. He had graduated and gotten a great job as a management trainee in a bank. I was taking catch-up summer school classes and working. I had gotten a great opportunity after my junior year to intern at the Department of Justice, which made me feel one step closer to taking on that international man of mystery role I secretly still coveted. Kevin and I would meet in a park on his side of town, play basketball or just sit in the car and drink a beer.

"This has got to be your line. You're going to be the dean of pledges next year," he said to me. "I'm gone, and now it's your turn. You are prepared for this."

I was happy that Kevin had my back, but I knew that, on some level, I was still fronting despite my confidence. Marc, Darryl, or others could be the DP if they wanted to. It didn't have to be me.

"I didn't get that ADP experience though. How is that going to affect things?"

"You got this. I mean, I got this. You have the drive. I have the institutional knowledge. This summer, we're gonna move the chapter forward. It's not about me anymore. I want to make sure you're good. You're gonna be baptized in your new role right now. You're going to have a lot of attention. You'll be the face of this magnificent-looking line, and there's going to be a lot of hype. You're gonna have to pull this thing off. I'm challenging you and I'm counting on you, but I'll be right by your side."

The whole summer was a mentoring exercise. Kevin wanted to ensure that I would be instilling the right values in the new line. It was a heroic effort.

Come fall, Kevin had set me up for success. I was ready to execute the vision we'd created together, and Marc and Darryl were on the roster as my ADPs. We were back on the yard, back in play, and the interest level was high. As part of the pledging process we called interviewing, interested young men would show up at our homes or dorm rooms to show their interest. They would often bring treats. My favorite was a bucket of KFC original recipe chicken and a two-liter bottle of Diet Pepsi (yes, Diet), and the dregs were littering my space. Hundreds of guys wanted to get in, and because we had dropped a year, we decided to double down for 1988. We selected thirty-one men, the largest line our chapter had ever had.

It was difficult—a very complicated process—not only to get the line going but to take care of myself. I was worried about this line, because the legacy of Kappa and our chapter was now in my hands.

On top of that, I was in my final year at Hampton. I was worried about graduating on time. I was thinking about the job I wanted after graduation. There was a lot riding on what I could manage, what I could do to hold it together in those last few months at Hampton.

WE HAD AN awesome coming-out party that year, and I mean awesome.

It was frigidly cold outside, but it didn't matter. The walk from the Emancipation Oak to the church was one of the proudest moments of my life.

Thousands came out to watch our thirty-one Scrollers make their debut after our year-long unintended hiatus. Their line name was Jalia. It was the largest line in the Beta Chi chapter's history, and I was the dean of pledges. I remember as we were finishing up our march around campus for the evening, Kevin came up to me and gave me a huge bear hug.

"You did it!" he said. "Do you understand the history you are making here?"

"We did it!" I responded immediately. "And yes, this *is* history we are making here. Thank you!"

I felt like Kevin was more excited than I was, because I was just keeping everything together. We would talk multiple times a week in the run-up to our debut. I kept him up-to-date on everything because I knew he would understand and offer the kind of support I needed. Every day that passed, I understood that this was still a hard assignment. Kevin wanted to come down one more time before the line crossed a few weeks later.

"Hey man, are you ready?" Kevin was on the phone. "Buttons and I are gonna drive down on Saturday afternoon after work. We'll be down for the night. We'll go to church the next day. We want to see the boys again before they cross."

"Cool! That's awesome."

More than anything, I never wanted to let Kevin down. I always wanted his approval. I always wanted his endorsement. I always wanted his acknowledgment. I was so happy.

But it wasn't cool. It wasn't awesome.

IT FELT LIKE a weird day. On February 6, 1988, I woke up feeling off my game. My stomach was just not right. I felt uneasy. I felt anxiety. I didn't know where it was coming from. All day, I was going through the motions.

That Saturday afternoon, there was a basketball game at Old Dominion. The Maryland Terrapins were coming down to play, and there were some high-profile players I knew on that team and wanted to see. A few friends were going to come along if Kevin and Buttons weren't, and I was their ride. I could see them waiting by my car. I looked at my watch and thought Kevin and Buttons would be down here by now, but it was still early in the afternoon, and I had Marc and Darryl doing the last-minute grunt work. I needed a break. I'd catch up to them later, calculating the hours in my head, knowing that it would still be early when we got back, well before we had to be with the line for the evening.

Driving back to campus later that day in the early evening, my sense of anxiety was off the charts. We weren't late, but as I pulled up into the yard, I could see one of my homegirls waving to me to pull over. As I did, I put the car into park and jumped out.

I could tell something was terribly wrong.

"What happened?" I asked, running up to her and the small group surrounding her.

"Oh, Derek," she said, looking at me with deep sadness in her eyes. "Kevin's been in an accident. He's dead. Buttons is okay, but Kevin, he's gone. We just heard."

Someone had hit Kevin's 1987 Volkswagen head-on at four thirty that afternoon, right as we were heading out to the game. As we were laughing in my car, his, heading south on I-95, was destroyed by a driver under the influence who had swerved through an embankment right into oncoming traffic at eighty miles an hour. Virginia state police found empty beer cans and a still-warm device for smoking marijuana on the passenger seat. The driver, at only twenty-two years of age, had an outstanding warrant for his arrest for failing to comply with a county drug education program at the time of his death in the collision with Kevin and Buttons. Kevin and Buttons had both been wearing seat belts. They had been driving safely. It wasn't their fault, but Kevin had paid for the accident with his life.

"Oh my God," I swore.

"Buttons is at Mary Washington Hospital," she offered. "They were only forty miles away when they crashed. We're going to go there now."

Buttons had already been transferred from the ER to a bed. When he regained consciousness, owing to his concussion he didn't even realize he had been in an accident.

My whole world was ripped apart. I was in shock, pain. My fraternity brother was dead, my mentor, my father figure, the one I had begun to count on. At age twenty-one, I was dealing with death for the first time. I was a wreck, but I was supposed to be a leader.

In that moment, time passed slowly and quickly. I could see the accident in my mind as the sparse details were shared. Everyone was going over what went wrong even though we had little to no information at the time.

Suddenly, there was a break in the conversation. Somebody was talking to me, at me. The voice hardly made it through the fog in my brain. Nothing was making sense.

"What time is it, Derek?"

"It's nine, nine in the evening."

"You gotta go, Brother. The line."

The line.

"I gotta go."

All I could hear in my head was the pounding of my responsibility. "You're the line leader. You know you have to leave, right? You gotta pull people together. Everybody's losing it right now. Get the line together."

Responsibility meant setting that night aside for talking about Kevin. We didn't walk out. We stayed up late, spent the time we needed sharing our memories of him. I spoke of my fondness for him, my love for him, and how he meant everything to me. And then we went to church the next day, as a group, to pray for him.

The funeral arrangements were made for the next week up in DC, and I was still under a lot of pressure. Some of the Nupes wanted to take the whole line up for the day, but I didn't want to force it. Most of the Brothers went up and a good number of the line, maybe half of them. The ones who pledged under him the previous year, the year we were shut down, they solemnly walked down the aisle and sat in silence. It was just sad. Kevin had a young child, two years old at the time, sitting between his mother and grandmother, not know-ing that he would never know his dad. It was rough, so rough that walking out of the church, I felt physically ill.

DEATH CLARIFIES things in a single moment. In a state of shock, there is a brightness, a laser-tight focus that brings everything into sharp relief: what matters, what doesn't, what has to be done, what can be left behind.

Before Kevin's death, I knew I had to step up, level up, and lead. After he died, I knew that with a greater intensity and sense of responsibility than I had ever felt before. At the same time, I didn't really understand on a gut level what lead-ership would mean for me, what it had to mean. To lead on my own without Kevin was unthinkable, unfathomable. In relative terms, I had only just met him. I had only just found someone I could trust, could look up to without hesitation, without fear that it would all fall apart.

After his funeral, I thought of all the moments when I had been in Kevin's exact situation, all of the moments when death was only a fraction of a second away.

During the same semester, around April, I had gone home for the weekend and decided to come back to school very early on Monday morning, so I left DC around four a.m. I was bone-tired, my head jerking up from the wheel as I continued to drift off to sleep right there on the same I-95 highway as I tried to make it back to campus. I don't know how I didn't veer off the road. On the way back to DC the previous school year, once again my tire had blown out on the highway in the left-hand lane. I had glided perfectly into the shoulder area, avoiding any swerving where I would have easily hit oncoming cars. Each time, things could've gone the wrong way. I might have been a headline in the newspaper the next morning, just like Kevin.

I should have gotten hit. I didn't get hit.

Faith has always been a personal thing for me. Like I said before, I wasn't raised in a religious home, but in reflecting on all of my near misses, I hoped, I knew, that He was guiding me. He's been there to alert me to what might otherwise destroy me. He put people around me to ensure that I was taken care of, a crew out there looking after me.

And by that I don't mean that God wasn't looking after Kevin. I'm not superhuman or divinely special. I attribute my survival, for the most part, to being damn lucky.

But when Kevin passed I recognized that, if I were to be the one who lived, I had to take this opportunity to really *be here*.

I could not pass by the opportunities I had to live.

I could not pass by the purpose I had to offer.

I could not pass by the faith I could put in God and, equally, in myself.

That realization was powerful.

Since that clarifying, painful, and powerful moment in which I lost my friend and mentor, I have known that every time I've been given a gift, it has a purpose. Kevin's legacy is that I am meant to convert each gift I receive into doing something good for somebody else.

I am alive, I am here, and I am willing.

6

PACESETTING

PEPSI SELLS itself, right?

Wanting to get myself on track and locked into a job, I let Pepsi know I was ready to sign by mid-April of 1988. After two interviews with the CIA, I was still waiting on news from them, and there was a big part of me that really wanted to be a secret agent. But Pepsi offered me a start date of June 6, only three weeks after my graduation from Hampton, and I said yes. I couldn't have been happier. I had secured a job in Baltimore as a sales management trainee. I was flying high.

I leaned into the Pepsi offer for a very specific reason.

Allen McKellar, born in 1920 in Abbeville, had graduated from the South Carolina Colored Agricultural and Mechanical College (now South Carolina State University) in 1940. Right out of the gate, he was hired by Pepsi-Cola as one of thirteen interns after winning an essay contest.

"We can still face the future with courage, with hope and with unbounded gratitude because America offers its youth an opportunity to face the dawn," he wrote.

McKellar became one of the first business professionals to break the color barrier in a major American corporation. His job was to promote Pepsi consumption in the Black community, but it was also a turning point in the American South. At the time, most hotels wouldn't accommodate Black salesmen, and some bottlers shunned them when they were trying to pick up their goods for delivery. A Pepsi executive even humiliated Black consumers by declaring publicly that the product was too good for them. With McKellar's essay, they decided to turn that around. Pepsi hoped its willingness to hire Black salesmen for prominent roles and to market directly to the Black community would give it advantages over its competitors, but it also was the right thing to do during a very difficult time in history.

Pepsi was willing to stand up for the Black community, and I felt like I could see myself standing up for them.

I didn't know what to expect my first day on the job, of course. I had spent the last four years as a student, imagining how I would become the man I wanted to be. Someone who had consequence in the world. There was a part of me that intrinsically believed I could do anything, and that's what I had counted on in attending Hampton: to always be prepared and ready to organize myself and others, set and achieve objectives, ramp up. But there was the other side of me as well, the one that didn't know if I could make my way outside university. Hampton was a small campus, a small community. Pepsi was anything but that.

The first thing I found out was that starting up in any mass-market management job isn't about sitting at a desk. Becoming accountable for sales means being present in stores, witnessing customer transactions, and taking care of what's on the shelves and displays. Whether you're at Pepsi or any other consumer products company, every day usually by seven a.m. (or six a.m. for me) you're on the road. Products and displays need to look pristine. Orders need to be plentiful.

More than anything else, I learned that you always have to be doing a slightly better job than your competitor. That means negotiating a prime spot in the store so that your product is the first thing a customer sees when they walk in. To do that, you have to build relationships with store managers and mom-and-pop owners so that you can keep expanding your products' footprint day in and day out.

"TOGETHER. EVERYONE. ACHIEVES. MORE," read my notes from my first day of training in all caps. "AND WINS," I scrawled underneath.

I sat in the room listening intently, looking around at the rest of the guys (and they were all guys on the sales team in the late '80s), writing as fast as I could. My notes ended up being half inspirational quotes, half metrics. Everything was measured, down to the last can of soda. The one goal was to meet my quota. Every day, every week, every month, every quarter, there were quotas to hit, and those quotas might change without a lot of notice.

Along with everyone else, I had been given two weeks to figure out the whole system, to learn what it took to run a solid Pepsi-Cola route. More than a few people were looking confused as we, the new hires, were given our first routes.

"Here's my pager number if you need me," my boss, Marc Bailey, said to me, handing me his card after my training ended. "But good luck, you know."

MY FIRST ROUTE was in inner-city Baltimore. I wasn't surprised about being assigned to a Black-majority route, but I was happy. I was excited about working this route because this was my turf, not that far from where I grew up. What was good for this community was good for me, and vice versa.

Instead of wearing a suit ready for an office, I was assigned what we called blues: a thick-fabric uniform designed to absorb and hide the worst of the spills when I was moving product off a pallet. Under that, I'd have my white Pepsi shirt and tie, but I learned very quickly that I'd be getting my hands dirty. I'd be driving those pallets around in something akin to an old ice cream truck, stuffed with what I'd need to fill sales for the day: my point-of-sale materials, a pricing gun and small equipment, and, on the passenger seat, the briefcase I'd been gifted at my graduation.

It wasn't like I was proud to be in the vehicle, a dated and frankly embarrassing piece of equipment. But I was proud of my job. It felt like a blue-collar environment. I knew, *no*, I hoped that there was a purpose in all of this. There was nothing better for learning the business from the ground level up than being on the ground.

But this team wasn't the Kappas. This wasn't the line. This wasn't a brotherhood. I could get left behind. Being at Hampton gave me all the tools that I needed. It helped. It lifted my confidence level higher. It gave me that social reinforcement that I belonged in an organization. But there were no more guarantees, and I had to get this right.

I always had a pricing gun in my hand. Back then, there were no automated systems or universal product codes, so part of my job was putting price stickers on everything I'd lug into stores. I'd look at the stickers clicking out of the gun: 99¢. Nine nine, nine nine, nine nine. I would tag two-liter bottles, I would tag sixteen-ounce non-returnables, spin-face everything. Put the point-of-sale placards up, put up the pole toppers with our current promotions. I would write up the orders. I'd work with the store personnel to keep their back rooms neat.

It was repetition, both the product work and the sales quotas. I just kept clicking.

My sales area wasn't exactly affluent. People didn't buy in bulk. There were certain times every month when food stamps and money became available for my customers, and that's when we moved product. Money on the street meant my quotas were filled. At the end of the month, everything turned slow, sluggish. Pepsi's expectations didn't change, but people didn't have the cash.

Right out of the gate, I was pushing really hard because I knew I had to show some real results. I was pushing the orders and pushing my store owners, but the product wasn't selling.

"Derek, we're not taking more product backlog before we have everything in the back of the shop sold," store managers would say to me. "Not gonna happen. If you send more product, I'm gonna refuse your orders, got it?"

Every quota felt like it was a battle because every number we aimed to reach was an aggressive stretch goal. Up until the last hour of that last day of each quota period, I was working to hit that number. We were running hard to the finish line every single month. If I made my number, I'd get the weekend off and return on Monday to bring that intensity back because by day three, day four, Marc or Jeff, the Director of Operations, would start asking questions about whether I'd make it. Those people who weren't making their numbers, they'd get held back a little bit later. Bosses might go out with them on their route. There were active interventions in play if you were any type of outlier.

I was out of ideas. My biggest worry was getting fired if I couldn't make those numbers. One Wednesday near the end of the month, I called Jeff.

"Hey, I'm having a problem with the quota. There's no money to be had. People here are just out of money. We gotta grind through and get to next week and then we'll be back in business. I'm really sorry. I hope I didn't let you down."

There was a pause on the other end of the line before he spoke.

"You're calling me to tell me about your numbers? Nobody does that. I've never had somebody call me and tell me this much detail. In fact, I've never had a trainee call me."

"Really?"

"Really. Derek, you're giving it your all, and I'm good with that. The results will be the results. Sometimes you're not gonna make your number. You and I are good."

"Are you sure? I feel like I let you down, let the company down."

"You know, if you spend your whole career here at Pepsi, you're gonna have periods where these types of things pan out this way for the right reasons. There are chances for you to overdeliver the next period and make up what you lost. But at your rate, your pace, and your intensity, you're gonna be fine. I don't want you to beat yourself up."

That was the moment I realized that I was putting more pressure on myself than my own boss. He was a very demanding boss, but I was even more demanding. I could not stop. If I did not stop, I could not lose.

ONE DAY, our sales team was called into a five a.m. meeting with regional vice presidents Nick and Tony who had just stopped in to see how we were doing. "Just stopping in" wasn't normal; it was a barely veiled threat. Obviously, there was something they wanted to talk to us about, something that we were not achieving to their expectations. If we were up to the job, they'd be invisible. At the time, there was a promotion for Diet Pepsi going on, and we were tasked with setting up new promotional racks in our stores. Every store needed at least one or two, three if you could hack it. Big promotion, big investment on the part of Pepsi meant big oversight.

"How's the promotion going?" The vice president spoke a little too loudly. I could see Jeff shake his head almost imperceptibly as he looked at upper management and then back to us, raising his eyebrows.

"How many rack placements do you have?" Another of the vice presidents nodded to the sales guy sitting next to him.

"One."

"You?" He turned to the next person at the table.

"Um, zero."

"Keep going."

"Two." "One." "Three."

And then he looked at me.

"Sixteen."

"You placed sixteen racks?"

"Yes."

"Sixteen racks."

"Yes." I shrugged.

Compared to the ongoing quota challenges, convincing stores to put up a few racks was simple in comparison. It was the least I could do. I'd been getting the racks set up just by telling store managers that we had a great promotion going on, a great price point, and some shiny new racks.

"Well, I know one thing for sure," he said, looking around. "There is one future vice president sitting in this room right now. The rest of you? Yeah, I have no idea."

Of course, after that meeting, all of the sales guys were giving me crap, as if I was showing them up on purpose. I never wanted to do that. Everyone could have been pacing me, but they weren't. They were cruising. I knew it and they knew it.

Theoretically, some of the guys on my team had an advantage in the suburban routes with their cleaner, nicer stores. But they had a much tougher battle to edge up over the kind of commitment I was able to build with my relationships in my own community. Even though I was in an inner-city neighborhood, Baltimore was a strong Pepsi market due in large part to the loyalty of Black consumers. The more I put in front of them, the more they were going to buy. That's why I was playing basketball with my store managers while other sales reps were hands-off. I was buying donuts for store personnel so that they'd trade me for favors when I needed them. I'd take the receivers in the back room out for beers or hand over Orioles tickets from Pepsi's partnership stash.

To me, I was doing what I thought was my job. To others, I was sending shockwaves through the Pepsi environment.

I was pulling in the numbers to make my bosses take notice. I got results.

I was building the relationships I needed to lift people up, to lift myself up, building tremendous rapport with people. I built trust and confidence in my community and received the same back.

And I was getting a reputation for high effectiveness. What I did stuck. Every sales report, I knew where I stood against my peers on other routes, and every week I pushed out the most product by talking to people, getting to know the community, and making sure every sale counted.

Within six months, I was promoted to a district manager position in a new sales department.

Like McKellar fifty years before me, I suddenly saw myself with the potential to work among the elite. McKellar set the pace for the Pepsi sales force. In his time, Pepsi encouraged McKellar to ride in luxurious Pullman train cars to get to his sales meetings, crisscrossing the country to pitch Pepsi by giving interviews and visiting schools, church groups, and mom-and-pop grocery stores. He landed Duke Ellington and other jazz stars for celebrity promotions. He also became one of the first Black vice presidents of a major corporation in the United States. I wanted that for myself. I hoped that I had it in me.

THE FIRST LESSON I learned at Pepsi was something I accepted as fact right there in that meeting: don't be afraid to be a pacesetter.

Being able to sell was all about setting a tone. For me, that tone was partnership. We were all in this together. We were all in this to make that next sale.

But even within the context of partnership, the ceiling was never the ceiling. That ceiling was always moving. Even when I knew I was at the head of the pack on that promotion, I didn't stop until there was no more rack space to secure. When I ran out of racks, I'd find new resources. Pepsi was a big company with lots of things to help me do my job. Promotional signs. Banners. Samples. Selling materials of all kinds. When I received a little expense account, I'd take a store manager to lunch. All this stuff was at my disposal, and I knew exactly what to do with my swag.

If you don't want to show up and get your hands dirty, and you're not excited about setting that pace, why are you in your current role?

For me, it felt good to win. To make my own job work, but better yet to make it easier for my customers, my community, and even for my bosses to win as well. That deal-after-deal-after-deal energy was something I didn't keep to myself. I shared it, even though I was only getting started, even though I was nervous that I wouldn't make it to my second month. I had my company's back, my community's back, and my own belief in building a future for myself.

What I discovered in those first six months at Pepsi was that I could create my own sense of belonging, and eventually the space for others to belong as well. I opened up our Pepsi community to the Black community, and vice versa. No longer written off as just the inner city, central Baltimore became a profit center. I didn't have to follow racialized social and performance norms and standards. Instead, I activated pacesetting for my peers.

And together everyone achieved more. We achieved excellence.

Just as I received my promotion letter, another letter arrived with a postmark from Virginia. The CIA had made me a job offer.

I kept that letter, but I politely declined.

I sold Pepsi now.

7

TRUST

ESS THAN eight weeks after I started at Pepsi in 1988, the
company sent around its race relations memo. By 1985,
Pepsi was aiming to be "The Choice of a New Generation," one that was reinvigorating its relationship with
Black communities, and yet the memo voiced the frustration
and isolation of Black Pepsi employees.

I have to credit Pepsi for trying. They were ahead of the
curve by a long way. Decades before corporations were paying
attention to diversity, equity, and inclusion, Pepsi took race
seriously. As Chair and CEO of PepsiCo from 1986 to 1996,
D. Wayne Calloway had launched the company's first effort
to change the performance-driven culture to one that focused
on "people development." He focused on tough issues such as
whether the company should pay for memberships to country clubs that excluded women. He personally committed to
leadership development for all of PepsiCo's employees and
served as a strong mentor for several executives, both men
and women and from different ethnic backgrounds.

Calloway also supported the creation of employee resource groups at PepsiCo. During this time, minority employees began to report strained relationships with managers and other employees. As a result, several employees at Pepsi formed the Black Managers Association (BMA). As the first recognized employee network, the BMA initially organized meetings where African American employees were able to meet and discuss their concerns and shared experiences. One of their first accomplishments was the development of a race relations program for Pepsi-Cola. All team members of all backgrounds were surveyed, and hundreds participated in interviews and focus groups, the results from which were listed in the memo, a document that verged on one hundred pages of authentic talk about race at Pepsi.

The memo suggested that racism was recognized as not just a social fact in the company but a deeply emotional issue cloaked in business justifications. Being white at Pepsi provided a social buffer, and being Black meant being seen as lacking in capabilities. Black team members believed that they had to be perfect, a cut above everyone else, if they were to succeed. White team members believed it too; they noticed and they cared.

We were all doing what we thought was our best. There was a lot of empathy, but there were not a lot of viable solutions to racism and racialization. The memo asked people to stand up, to say something, to protect each other, to act instead of standing by. But the lived reality of doing the right thing was a lot harder than that.

Even within the ranks of Black employees at Pepsi, we didn't know how to support each other when race was in the works. And that's why not all of my relationships within the company worked as well as the one I had developed with Jeff.

THREE YEARS after I started with Pepsi, there was a lot of competition over who would be the next General Manager (GM) in our Washington, DC, operation after the current boss, Graham, retired. Graham was white, and I had just begun to work for a new sales manager myself, Troy. Troy was one of the very few Black men being considered for that GM role, and he seemed genuinely committed to making some positive changes for our team. The management team in this location was predominantly Black.

Early on after we got started together, I was coming out of a meeting with Troy when I was pulled aside by Graham.

"Hey, what's going on? Derek, how's it going?"

"I just got out of a meeting with Troy."

"What did you guys talk about?"

I gave Graham some tidbits of what Troy had proposed. Innocently and excitedly, I was hyped up about Troy's new ideas for sales compensation. But this was not a deep dive. My conversation with Graham took less than sixty seconds.

"Okay, that's good. That's good to know. Alright. Well, good seeing you."

And that was it.

Graham didn't give me any indication that he was disenchanted or surprised by anything I said. He seemed as excited as I was. But within twenty-four hours, something had changed with Troy. His whole temperament with me had shifted. He had always been smiling, happy, and calm, and then the very next day, yeah, he didn't say anything to me at all. There was an unexpected chill in the air.

I couldn't, at the beginning, pinpoint why Troy was being short with me, and I was surprised. I assumed he was simply in a different kind of mood that day, until he broke the ice.

"The next time you talk to my boss about something, I'd like a heads-up."

"Oh, sorry," I said, stumbling over my words. "I didn't, you know, I didn't run right to him and tell him that. I bumped into him in the hallway walking out of the meeting. He's the boss and he asked me a question, and I answered the question. I didn't volunteer the information."

"No."

"I apologize, Troy."

But it didn't matter. In his mind, I had betrayed him. I was the Uncle Tom on the team, sucking up to the white guys, the white bosses. Taken from Harriet Beecher Stowe's novel *Uncle Tom's Cabin*, it's what we call those among us who give up or hide their Blackness, traits, and practices in order to be accepted into the white mainstream. I was the furthest thing from an Uncle Tom in my mind. I was the HBCU guy. The Chocolate City guy. I was talking him up to Graham, not taking sides. I couldn't understand it.

From that moment on, Troy went out of his way to leave me on the sidelines. The narrative he was creating alienated me from my peer group. I could tell that the tenor of my relationships had changed; they were situating me as an outsider now. I still had some members of my team that I had brought in myself whom I could trust, but that blackball status meant that most of the inroads I had gained in my new role with Troy were now blocked.

I lacked access to Troy himself as well. Most of my conversations with him took place within a short five-minute window.

"What do you need, Lewis?"

"Well, I need some pricing authorizations."

"Why don't you go talk to the GM. If I were you, I would just go talk to him about it. Like you do everything else."

Troy didn't give me an inch. He didn't allow me to repair our relationship. He put a wall up and created all these new rules. Everybody had to be in at five a.m., and if we didn't make it, we were late. It was affecting everybody, this grudge of his, trying to catch me out. But I was up for the challenge. I was fine. I was there at four thirty a.m., and I would watch our team members rushing, racing to get in there at 4:59, tired as hell.

It was a mental challenge to keep doing my job, getting out there fighting, driving sales. But when I was out in the market working closely with my team and our customers, I was in my element, I was fine. I was grinding. I was doing my job to the best of my ability, and I was focused.

Graham retired, as everyone expected. But to Troy's surprise, he didn't get tapped for the GM job. They brought in someone new, someone white, someone from our primary competitor.

Jim Schultz's objective was to accelerate business performance, and my job was to keep my head down and do what I do best. I kept playing my own game. I was still getting there early. I was out in the yard. I was in stores. I was meeting with customers. I was still hustling, solving problems, and making things happen. Troy was very obviously disappointed he didn't get the job. You could see it took some energy out of him. So while Troy was still trying to battle me a little bit, he also looked embarrassed that he didn't get the big job. And when Jim would ask questions in team meetings, I had the answers because I was in the middle of everything.

Now Troy was fighting a different fight.

I saw what was happening, the writing on the wall.

And I had his back. I reached out to Troy every chance I could. "Hey, the GM called me.".

"Jim asked me about something."

"I'm letting you know what numbers I'm giving Jim today, and I'm giving them to you too."

There were details in the business that only I knew, and I had an opportunity in front of me to help the whole team. Troy was floundering, and I had the chance to right some wrongs. Yes, he had closed that door early in our relationship, but I learned that I should have been offering up this approach all along.

One day soon after, Troy came to me.

"I want to go out and ride with you. We're gonna go out into the market, spend a whole day together."

"Wow, yeah, okay, Troy. Let's do that."

We were having a really good conversation. He was nice to me. He was laughing, telling jokes and stories almost as if nothing had ever happened. I felt, "This is good. This is what I always wanted it to be. Maybe we're getting into a rhythm now."

Then while we're out there that day, Jim calls me while I'm in the car with Troy.

"Hey, I need you back for a quick huddle session at five o'clock. Okay?"

"Okay. Alright."

"Who was that?" Troy asked when I hung up.

"It was Jim."

"What'd he call for?"

"He wants me back for a meeting."

"What is the meeting about?"

"He didn't say."

I walked into Pepsi, and my name was already in the air.

"Derek Lewis. Call 4871. Derek Lewis, 4871," the intercom pinged across the whole warehouse.

I went into Jim's office, and there are already two peers of mine in the room.

"I just wanted you guys to know I just let Troy go. And now you all report directly into me. And that's it."

I looked around the room. I was shocked. Jim had powerful observation skills, and it hadn't taken him long to understand whom he could trust.

AIMING FOR PERFECTION was something that I knew well.

Living that high expectation I set for myself at home, at school, and at Hampton had kept me safe. It had kept me on a trailblazing path. I was comfortable in that place of proving that I was able to succeed. The juxtaposition of having to prove myself and actually delivering excellence was worth the philosophical nuance. I had recognized that even delivering a little more effort than expected of me was going to drive the outcomes that I wanted for *myself*, not just for Pepsi.

Making that effort meant something, something real and something effective, when it came to my relationships within the company.

But I didn't do everything right. Trust has to go in both directions. Despite Troy's limitations, I was at fault for my failure to see the full picture. It was my job to let him know what was going on. I didn't make that mistake intentionally. But I soon came to recognize the implications of what I had done and how that made my boss feel.

I had inadvertently made Troy feel disempowered, not only as a boss but as a Black man. At that time within the company, people like Troy did not have the same lived experience as white managers. They didn't have the same access to the white management team as white managers. Their role was mainly all Black workforce management. Troy didn't have a high level of trust for white leadership for good reason. People in Troy's role saw good people get fired for simple slipups. And Troy felt like I was declaring that I wanted to be on the white side of the fence versus being on his side.

Race complicated things; it still complicates things. Even with all of the commitment to race relations at Pepsi, neither the BMA nor Calloway had found a way to make diversity an organizational priority among PepsiCo's largely autonomous and decentralized operating units in the early '90s. Our team was emblematic of that essential problem. Calloway's approach was not programmatically linked to diversity practices nor to the company's business strategy, and we were all fending for ourselves despite everyone's best intentions.

In my experience with Troy, I learned the value of managing up and having authentic relationships with the people around me. I learned to apologize, even for unintentional mistakes. I learned to give my bosses a heads-up on conversations so that they heard *about* me *from* me, first and always. I learned to think about my bosses as people, and as people I wanted to form a relationship with deliberately. I'm glad Jim trusted me, but Troy should have been able to trust me as well.

Work does not have to be *just* transactional. We spend every day with the people in our workplace, and we communicate with them.

We need to trust each other, and trust ourselves, enough to have difficult conversations, conversations that may end in more questions.

It doesn't have to go perfectly.

To trust is a choice, an act of authentic communication, and a commitment to integrity. To trust means that we are open to hearing others' pain points. To trust means that we believe in who we are and how we're showing up to make tomorrow that much better.

8

SHERENE

T WASN'T JUST that I already had a girlfriend when I met Sherene back at Hampton in September 1987. It was my senior year. I was elected to serve as dean of pledges for the spring '88 Kappa line. I was also elected to serve as Mr. Business Club. And it was the year I began interviewing for my first professional job. Sherene, or any other young woman in my midst at the time, wasn't on my radar.

And yet from the moment I met her, Sherene was the kind of memorable woman that you don't let go of, not if you know what's good for you.

I had pulled up to Virginia-Cleveland Hall, a women's dorm, with a friend, Marc, in my white Ford Escort. As a courtesy from our Kappa crew, we were escorting frosh to their first off-campus mixer on Labor Day weekend. That wasn't a euphemism. We wanted to keep the younger students safe. With frosh who were unused to super late nights, unfamiliar spots, and alcohol, especially right out of high school, we weren't aiming to get anyone in trouble. We just wanted to show off our chapter.

Marc spotted three young women sitting on their stoop and jumped out of the car.

"What are you guys doing tonight?"

"Nothing. It's too hot," one of them said. "We're just sitting here in the shade."

"Wanna go to a Kappa party?"

"Wait a minute. I got a boyfriend," I heard one of the women say. "Up at the University of Maryland. I don't even know you guys. You know, I don't wanna talk to any other guys."

"Come on, Sherene, I'm bored," said another.

"Yeah, Sherene, let's go."

"Alright, okay. Okay. But I'm, you know, just gonna be faithful to my boyfriend. I'm just saying."

I said nothing. I was just the driver. And the first woman was right: it was too hot. I don't know why I was wearing my Kappa jacket in that car. But Marc got back in the front, the three young women squeezing into the back seat, no seat belts.

I don't remember that much about the party itself. I noticed that Sherene was having a good time. I wasn't drinking as I was on escort patrol, and I had to drive a lot of younger students back to their rooms. Most of them had a midnight curfew, so it was a rush to coordinate everyone at the last minute. Sherene looked panicked as I came back in the room after one of my rounds, and I could hear her talking to her friends.

"It's eleven thirty. We gotta get back. I don't know how far away we are."

"We'll be fine." Her friend nodded at her. "We'll just call somebody and tell them to open the side door right to let us in."

The problem with that plan was that 1987 was well before cell phones, and even though we called from the party and then stopped at a pay phone at a gas station to call again, nobody answered the phone in the dorm's hallway. They had no way of getting back in, and they were looking at me.

"Alright, we can work this out. I'm driving you to my place."

"You are not driving us to your place," Sherene said.

"I am. I am. You all can stay in my bedroom, and I'll sleep downstairs on the sofa," I assured them. "I'm a nice guy."

"You'd better be a nice guy," one of the other young women said. "And you'd better have some food. I'm hungry."

We were all hungry. I had some frozen pizzas. Sherene set the dial and put the pizza in the oven, and we forgot about it a little bit and it came out a little crusty. In the morning, I dropped them off.

"Here's my number if you guys ever need anything, right?" I said as I turned back to the car. "You know, I can give you a ride somewhere or whatever. Hope you guys are good."

I watched them casually saunter into their dorm as if they had been there the whole night and then out for an early morning breakfast.

It wasn't even twelve hours later when I got a call from Sherene's roommate.

"Everyone here's gone away for the weekend," she said. "Are you doing anything?"

I could hear giggling in the background. My girlfriend was also off campus because classes hadn't even started up yet, and to me, these young women were like my little sisters more than competitors for my affection.

"Yeah, I'm not doing anything right now. There is a party over in Norfolk I'm headed to later. I'll come by and pick you guys up." I laughed.

When I arrived, I could see the other women forcing Sherene into the front seat for some reason, while they took up the whole of the back. She seemed both confused and embarrassed, looking down at her lap or out the window. From my vantage point, the ladies in the back seemed to be pointing and waving in my rearview mirror, communicating something complicated to me that I didn't quite understand. Sherene would turn around when she noticed the movement and they would stop.

One of them took the lead. "Can you drop us off here, Derek?"

"Oh sure," I said. "I thought we were all going to do something together?"

"I mean, yeah, but I have to stop here," she said sincerely. "I forgot we were meeting someone, um, like, now?"

I pulled over only ten minutes after we started driving.

"So," I looked at Sherene, smiling, "do you want to go get something to eat?"

Sherene and I never really dated at Hampton that semester. We kept in touch. But it was the kind of keeping in touch that involved late night phone calls, secret messages left on dorm room doors, and not quite truthfulness on my part. It seemed that Sherene had dropped her Maryland boyfriend.

I didn't tell Sherene anything about my girlfriend, whom I had been dating since the previous school year. I thought simply telling her I had one was enough information. At twenty years old, whether I was right or wrong, I thought I had checked all of the appropriate information-sharing boxes.

It wasn't until homecoming later that fall that Sherene realized that she wasn't the only one in the picture. That night I escorted my official date to the homecoming coronation as Mr. Delta Sigma Theta, and boy, was everyone watching, including Sherene and her friends. Some people knew that I had been spending time with her, and some didn't. But enough people knew that it didn't feel right to be taking that walk with another woman on my arm.

I knew that my actions would not sit well with Sherene.

I knew, despite the fact that I had given her the heads-up about my other relationship, that I hadn't given her the truth, the whole truth, and nothing but the truth. The truth was that I felt conflicted. I had strong feelings for Sherene. We clicked on many levels, and I wanted things to continue. So I kept playing along with the status quo, knowing at some point this situation was going to implode. It was not as if I wanted to see things blow up. I didn't. I kept telling myself I needed to clean it up before things got ugly.

But I waited too long.

February 14, 1988, is the day I like to call the Hampton Valentine's Day Massacre.

I was at home with my girlfriend when I got a knock at the door. Sherene had decided to have it out with me, and her voice carried through the hallway. No more hiding or deflecting. It got ugly, as I knew it would. At the end of that conversation, Sherene and I were done, and not surprisingly, it was the beginning of the end with my girlfriend too.

I never wanted to hurt anyone, but I did. I felt terrible about it.

Eventually I convinced myself that I didn't care.

There was a lot going on in my world. With schoolwork, pledging, and interviewing for jobs, I was moving on and getting ready the next chapter of my life. Kappa was as strong as ever on campus, and I did the work I promised to do as DP. I was consistently interviewing and landing job offers, with four offers on the table going into April. My classwork load was getting easier by the week; for the entire second semester, my classes were only on Tuesdays and Thursdays, so I had lots of free time, maybe for the first time since I had arrived at Hampton.

As much as I thought I was over Sherene, I really wasn't. At the same time, I knew I could not turn around and try to get her back, at least right then. I knew that I was going to be moving into my first professional job, and my career wasn't going to be centered in the quiet corner of Virginia where Sherene would be at school for another three years. I did not feel good about trying to nurture a long-distance relationship. I knew how hard it would be on both of us, and I didn't think it was fair to either one of us, even if she would deign to take me back.

My priority had to be my career, not a relationship. Nothing was going to negatively affect that, I told myself. So I deprioritized serious relationships with women altogether. It gave me comfort because I could focus on gearing up for my first adult job, and I liked the simplicity of not having to worry about anyone else.

But as the months went by and I was inching ever closer to my final days at Hampton, every time I turned the corner on campus, I saw Sherene. She wouldn't even look in my direction.

I graduated without knowing where we stood or if we'd ever see each other again.

I HAD MOVED BACK TO DC and came back down to Hampton about twice a year: once for homecoming with Kappa, and once for Career Day.

In 1991, I began to recruit and interview seniors on behalf of Pepsi, just as I had been recruited only a few years earlier.

I didn't know how truly personal recruiting would get. The company had taken my picture to send ahead for the Hampton

Me at six years old in 1973

TOP: Me (age seven) and my brothers Damon (two) and Butch (eight months)

BOTTOM: My sixth grade class photo; I had turned eleven in January

TOP: My graduation day at Hampton University in Hampton, VA, in 1988.
L to R: My aunt Joannie, me, and my aunt Carolyn
BOTTOM: Mom, me, my son Devon (age three), Damon, and my long-lost
sister at my Xavier University MBA graduation in Cincinnati, OH, in 1998

TOP: Scroller Club coming-out party on campus in January 1986
LEFT: Stepping hard on the yard with the Nupes back in fall 1987
RIGHT: Overseeing Hell Week activities for the spring 1988 line, Jalia

TOP: Hamptonians gathering at the Lewis residence for an Orlando Alumni Chapter event. L to R: President Darrell K. Williams; First Lady Myra Williams; my son Kellan; my wife, Sherene; and me

LEFT: Hanging with Pepsi legends Allen McKellar (center) and Maurice Cox in St. Louis in 2016

RIGHT: Me and legendary Hampton University President Dr. William Harvey at HU's annual gala in 2018

TOP: Team Lewis hanging together at the NBA Finals in Miami to support the Heat as they win the title in 2013

BOTTOM: Devon's Senior Day at Georgetown University. L to R: My mom, Barbara; me; Devon; Sherene; and my mother-in-law, Patricia

TOP: Celebrating my daughter, Jordan, at Baylor WBB's Senior night and the team's Big 12 Regular Season Championship win in Waco, TX, in 2022
BOTTOM: Kellan's Senior Day at Lake Highland Preparatory School in February 2024

TOP: Me playing in an official LPGA golf tournament, Hilton Tournament of Champions, with NFL HOF Charles Woodson (second from left) and LPGA Professional Stacy Lewis (third from left) while Devon was my caddy
LEFT: Me playing golf at Carnoustie Golf Links in Scotland in 2014
RIGHT: My first and only hole in one I achieved in Bermuda in 1997

TOP: Me playing at Pebble Beach Golf Links in Monterey, CA, in 2022
LEFT: Sherene and me flanking the Wanamaker Trophy at the 2021 PGA Championship
RIGHT: Enjoying teatime and tennis together at The Championships, Wimbledon

TOP: Me (far left) and other Pepsi campus hire Hamptonians posing for a campus recruiting picture in fall 1988

BOTTOM: Pepsi's Team Elite South Division leadership team en route to conduct market visits in February 2019

TOP: Me speaking to media in Atlanta, GA, regarding a joint initiative with Pepsi, Shaquille O'Neal (right), and the Sheriff's Offices in Fulton and Henry Counties

BOTTOM: Me hanging with Pepsi's Historically Better Gala VIP guests Naturi Naughton (center) and Terrence J in Washington, DC

TOP: Speaking to a classroom of students at the Culverhouse College of Business at the University of Alabama in 2019

BOTTOM: Holding a huddle session with the Norfolk State University's (VA) men's basketball team during their fall camp in 2022

TOP: Cohosting the Mid-Level Managers' Symposium with Dr. Randal Pinkett at the Executive Leadership Council's annual gala in 2022
BOTTOM: Chilling with the Nupes at a Hampton vs. Howard football game in Washington, DC, in 2015

FACING TOP: Me and Sherene with John Legend at the Florida Hospital Foundation's (now AdventHealth's) Golden Gala in 2018

FACING MIDDLE: Me, Sherene, and A.J. Calloway with New Edition

FACING BOTTOM: Kicking it with Migos at NBA All-Star weekend in Charlotte, NC, in 2019

TOP LEFT: Me and Kellan with Flo Rida at the NFL Pro Bowl in Orlando, FL

TOP RIGHT: Me, Mary J. Blige, and Don Pooh at Brooklyn Chop House

BOTTOM LEFT: Hanging with my great friend Doug E. Fresh at a Hampton Homecoming event

BOTTOM RIGHT: Catching some BIG3 hoops action with Ice Cube

Sherene and me attending the 1993 Presidential Inaugural Ball
in Washington, DC

events shortly after I was a campus hire, and when I walked on campus, there was a big poster of me right in the front of the college Career Center with the slogan "Recruiting a New Generation of Leaders." Inside the center were tables, chairs, and little interview pods for privacy. I unloaded our swag at the Pepsi table along with my colleague, Mike, right next to the guys from Mars and a few pods down from the Department of Justice. We had a fantastic day. We spoke with hundreds of students. We collected dozens of high-caliber résumés. We had a line of sight to the next generation of future leaders in our company.

It was a Thursday night. After working hard the entire day, Mike and I decided it was time to play. We were staying overnight; we weren't heading back home until the morning.

There was a local club nearby, one where Hampton students would kick off their weekend. Mike and I decided that that was the spot. Maybe I would know a few people from back in the day, and it would be a great opportunity to reconnect, even make some business connections. We got there, and it turned out I recognized several people there.

One of those people was Sherene.

Ironically, while Mike and I were driving down to Hampton for the event a day earlier, I had told him about Sherene, about our missed connection. I don't know what made me bring it up. I guess I knew she was still in school there, and I knew there was a likelihood I'd see her somewhere around campus.

Mike's intuition was on point.

"It sounds like you still like this young lady," he said. "What are you prepared to do when you see her?"

"I don't know. I've spotted her on campus before, but never close enough to say anything to her. I know she was in a relationship, so I didn't want to get in the middle of that."

Every time I saw Sherene's face in my mind, I made the decision to move on from any thought of approaching her. But this time something felt different, almost as it if was divine.

In the club, Sherene and I made eye contact. She gave me one of those cold looks, a what-are-*you*-doing-here look. I was disappointed but not surprised. I had done everything and then some to deserve it.

I pointed out Sherene to Mike.

"She ain't feeling me, brother," I said.

Mike nods, turns away from me, and heads over to Sherene's side.

"I gotta tell you something," he said to her, nodding his head back toward me. "My dude wore my ear out the entire ride from DC. *Sherene, Sherene, Sherene.* I just had to meet her."

"What?" she asked, her face confused.

"He is over there. Like, crying in his beer. You won't even say three words to him. Would you at least speak to him and say hello? Like, please just do that? Because I cannot do this ride back tomorrow knowing that you guys did not talk."

Smiling, Mike walked straight back over to me.

"Oh, shit."

"No shit! If she comes up to you, you talk to that woman!"

There was a lot going on. To be honest, just as everything was coming together at work, I was still working things out with myself. The end of my relationship with my college girl-friend, which happened a few months before Career Day, was really one of attrition. She was working in one city, and I was in another once I got promoted to my role in Washington, DC. A forty-five-minute drivable distance, but not a sustainable one given that we didn't seem to be on the same page. I had started hanging out with other young ladies in the DMV, but nothing really felt right.

Sherene did not come up to me, so I took courage from Mike's audacity and decided I would go up to her.

"Are you doing the recruiting thing? Do you have a favorite company? How are you doing? What's been going on? What have you been up to?" I was already talking too much.

"Yeah, no," she said. "I gotta go."

"I really would like to, you know, just connect with you one time, just to talk and catch up. You know, you're doing great. Getting ready to graduate. You're all grown up."

"Derek, I take offense to that. I was never a child."

"Well, I'd like to call you sometime," I stumbled.

"Sure. Well, no. Maybe not right now. I'm just not there. I am just being honest with you."

"I got that," I admitted. "I get that. Hopefully, I'll see you again."

"Good for you," she said.

SHERENE KNEW her worth, and she held her ground. Later, when I got to know her better, I understood where that worth had come from. Sherene's extended family was large, close, and supportive. It wasn't a matter of her family's economic or social status alone, although those were factors in the differences between our childhoods. Sherene's family had a sense of collective purpose and value that made it seem like someone would always be there to hold her if she fell. She knew that she had choices in life, and she wasn't at all willing to get into a relationship in which she would feel second best or like an afterthought.

After Career Day, Sherene and I actually had a chance to talk. A lot of my old feelings for her started to cascade within me from the moment I sat down with her, finally catching my breath after years of holding her as an image in my mind.

I knew that I had always liked her, but it was different when she was about to graduate university and I was fully committed to my career, having just turned twenty-four. It was different because she was even better than I remembered, than I expected her to be. All of a sudden, comparing Sherene with every other woman that I had dated, I still had her at number one. It could only be her. She was by far the best person I had spent time with, and still is, to this day. And I said to myself, "If there's a chance to get back with her, then I'm gonna go for it."

Knowing Sherene's worth, I also began to see my own. As we started dating officially, I recognized how far I had come since I was twenty-one, full of confidence but never sure of myself. I recognized that by hedging my bets, I had been setting myself up for failure.

I couldn't make a decision about Sherene earlier, not because I couldn't see her value but because I couldn't see my own.

I needed to see the foundation within myself and stand by my principles in order to find a relationship that would allow me to thrive. In that way, Sherene's story is very much integral to my story and to my personal growth since we met.

Once that relationship was established, there could be no going back. I'm not saying that we never had our issues, Sherene and me, but together we created a team that allowed us to build from commitment, not toward it. The commitment we have to our team, to each other and our whole family's best interests, has and always will come first. The richness that comes from that relationship is not about how much we can give to each other but how well we can continuously live a values-oriented life side by side.

In a partnership, it's really important to have someone who is on the same trajectory as you are. I don't expect Sherene to fulfill all of my needs. I expect her to be the best version of herself, and I expect the same of myself.

We're both in the same race but wearing the same colors, competitive with each other and drafting off each other, crossing the finish line together.

9

SISTER

WHEN I WAS in my early teens, I often did chores for my grandparents, cleaning their house and mowing the lawn. It was part of growing up in an extended-family environment. We did for each other. But it also meant I could bring home a little extra cash, especially when it came to my aunts. They were both working women, but still living at home because they weren't married. I would go into their rooms and collect their laundry, wash, dry, and iron it all. Every extra five dollars I earned meant that I could buy a new pile of comic books.

But once in a while, my work around the house could more accurately be called snooping around.

My grandparents' home was comforting and kind, and it was my second home, especially when I was a young boy. Their well-built house, on a quiet and leafy lot, was also full of secrets, both intentional and not. I can remember touching the spines on my grandparents' books, looking at the art they had collected over the years, absentmindedly leafing through old church newsletters left on a desk, and checking their closets for hidden birthday presents.

As I was snooping one day, I started going through the family albums, those old creaky books of photographs we had printed at the pharmacy. The ones where you pulled back the cellophane pages to place each picture on a gummy white surface, hoping it would stay in place. Flipping through our collective family history, I found a picture of a teenage woman in a gown looking like a debutante. "Yeah, my mom sure was pretty," I thought to myself as I took the picture over to my aunt to show it to her. My mom was cool.

"I found a picture of Mom in an evening dress. Was this from her prom?" I said, holding it out for her to see.

"Sweetie, that's not your mom," she said.

"What do you mean?"

I got a look from my aunt that I didn't expect. That we-need-to-talk look.

"Derek, that's your sister."

"My what?"

She was my full sister. My mom and Roland had started early, and Sister was born two years before me. Mom had to give her up when she was sixteen, a requirement by my grandparents, for both the right and the wrong reasons.

The wrong reason, at least by today's standards, was that it just didn't look right. At the time, it was probably the right call. The fate of a too young unwed mother was something that needed to be avoided in the 1960s, both for her own good and for my grandparents'. My grandparents also did not have the time nor the energy to bring up a child while my mother was finishing high school.

And they made sure she finished. The right reason was that my grandparents wanted my mom to go to university.

She was bright and she was being prepared for that one step further, the step beyond what they themselves had achieved. Even though Roland's handiwork meant that Mom was pregnant again before she graduated high school, my grandparents believed in her abilities and her future.

In any case, my sister ended up adopted into a Jehovah's Witness family from Buffalo. Abortion was out of the question, but there were always good people ready to step up to adopt beautiful babies.

Mom didn't know where Sister was sent after her birth, but my grandparents always knew her whereabouts, even years later—a fact I figured out before Mom was aware. In finding that picture, I saw my sister as a teenager well before my mom or Roland did.

After that bomb was dropped, I was sworn to secrecy.

"You can't tell her you saw this picture," my aunt said.

From that moment on, we just didn't talk about it. I was holding on to that secret, all on my own, for two years. I never brought it up to anyone, even the people who knew I knew, like my aunts and, I assume, my grandparents.

When I was sixteen, Mom finally told me.

"I think I know you know already," she said, having talked to her mom and the family about it.

It was a good conversation, not an emotional one. Mom just shared the facts.

"I'm gonna go find her," I said.

I didn't, at least not right away. I reached out to my sister around the time I graduated high school, but I didn't actually meet her until she showed up at my college graduation.

MY SISTER is one of the missing parts of my heart.

At the time we met, it felt like a slow fade into a film already halfway through the action. Our relationship has felt the same way ever since. We seem to circle and move in and out of each other's lives, zooming in and out of frame.

Around the time the COVID-19 pandemic began, it felt like we were starting to jell. We were having a family video chat every couple of weeks, all of us, including Mom, my brother Damon, Sherene, and sometimes our kids would jump in on the call. We kept the momentum rolling.

But suddenly, we lost contact with her. She didn't show up one week, or the next. Mom may have made things a bit more difficult because, fearing a second loss of the child she once had to give away, she became frantic. She called people my sister knew, rang up at her job. On one level, it was intrusive. But on another level, Mom was trying to do right by Sister and make sure she was okay. It was the pandemic, after all.

We know that something had happened for Sister. Something one of us said bothered her. We know that her version of faith and belief was different from ours because of the way that she was raised. For whatever reason, she needed to stop talking to us.

To me, it was a bigger loss than perhaps Sister realized. My youngest brother had been murdered, and now she had gone AWOL on the family. It wasn't the same, but the feelings I carried inside me were similar.

At the core of my response was one simple thing, namely the recognition that I was a part of a dysfunctional family.

When it comes to my family, we're not talking about the regular ebbs and flows of life. We're talking about a group of people who, at many points in their existence, were barely hanging on to life and to each other. When we weren't, we didn't always know how to connect, how to talk to one another openly, vulnerably.

We were almost there. We were *so close*. And yet we weren't. Not at all.

I grew up in a household that could have been a happy family of six people: a husband and a wife and four lovely children. And yet we never ever, ever, *ever* got a chance to spend time together as six. We didn't even spend time together, before I knew about my sister, as five, or even as four after Roland left for good. And then we lost Butch.

There's only really been the three of us who have been plugging along together.

Psychologically, because I perceived myself to be the oldest child in my family, I had felt a sense of responsibility to my siblings. When my sister emerged out of the ether, I wondered how much we would have in common. Would we be alike? Would she replace me in the eyes of my brothers? Would sharing her existence be seen as airing dirty laundry?

But none of those questions really mattered. I knew I always wanted a sister. In my young mind, when I first discovered her photo, I immediately thought that we would have been perfect together, laughing and sharing secrets like Damon and Butch used to do because they were so close in age. Sister and I were only a couple of years apart, just like them. She could have been my confidante, my best friend.

The reality of knowing her was very different, and not because she was lacking in any way. We vibed. We could tell that we had a natural connection. We could both feel the potential.

But Sister's background was so very different, and so the way she thought was foreign to me. Growing up in the northern part of New York state on the border of Canada, she didn't know what it was like living on the border of the South, born just after the Civil Rights Act had come into play. Our cultures were different; our beliefs were different. The connections we each made in our neural pathways between past and present, faith and knowledge, were so unalike.

It was almost as if there was an invisible barrier between us. We were so close, but there was also too much time, too much circumstance, too much distance forcing us apart, eroding all of the chances we had to build a connection.

SOMETIMES FAMILIES are places of deep comfort and compassion, and sometimes family life just doesn't work out the way we want it to. We all know that. But as much as we know this to be true, it doesn't mean it won't hurt.

"Damn, why? Why?" I would think to myself every time I remembered my personal losses, of Butch, of Sister. "Here we go again."

In my case, the fact that we're blood relatives didn't matter in the end. In my siblings' cases, with the exception of Damon, our shared genetic memory didn't provide us with a permanent bond. It's the same thing for many of us. Family can be wonderful, but it is not a guarantee of anything in life. In some of our lived experiences, family itself is what we survive. There are so many of us who have been let down by our family experiences, whether due to separation, divorce, abuse, or loss of any kind. Why didn't we get this life together? Why didn't we have a chance to do family the right way? It was nobody's fault. It's how it all came together. But Sister was robbed, and I was robbed, of being part of each other's lives.

I have learned to think about family as an airplane in flight. You want to get to forty thousand feet because it's safer, faster, calmer up in the highest highs, gliding at altitude. But some rides never get past ten thousand. Some never get off the ground. Sometimes, you're sitting in the plane waiting for that feeling of liftoff, and it never happens. Unless you're an airplane engineer, you'll probably never know the reason why your flight got canceled.

Eventually you'll have the ability to disembark and choose a different destination, even if that destination is just driving back to the office. You can also choose to get to the same destination more slowly.

Thinking about what could have happened, what never happened, isn't going to get you there. You have to set your sights on where you want to go, find a map to get you on the road, and get yourself in gear.

10

THIRTY SUITS

EARL G. GRAVES SR. and Earvin "Magic" Johnson Jr. purchased the Pepsi-Cola bottling franchise in Washington, DC, in 1990. I'm pretty sure that everyone reading this book knows who Magic Johnson is, given that he was the superstar of the LA Lakers when he bought into Pepsi, but whether or not you've heard of him, Earl Graves ought to be just as famous. Graves started out in politics in the 1960s as Senator Robert F. Kennedy's administrative assistant. Shortly after Kennedy was assassinated, Graves went into business for himself and founded *Black Enterprise* magazine, for which he lobbied and received a $175,000 loan in 1970, backed by advertising contracts he had secured through his own hard graft. He became a bestselling author with his book *How to Succeed in Business without Being White: Straight Talk on Making It in America*, still in print today. Achieving at the highest level, he built a multimillion-dollar empire and wanted to show Black entrepreneurs that they could have all of their dreams fulfilled. *All* of their dreams—not only the small and insignificant ones, but also the biggest, most audacious dreams possible.

"I was just another entrepreneur who believed in himself," Graves said to an interviewer from *The Post-Standard* in Syracuse, New York, in 2005. "The only difference was that I was Black."

I was promoted back up to Washington, DC, from Maryland to work for Magic and Graves, but a year and a half earlier back in Baltimore, I had rented an apartment in West Baltimore. And in that countdown to moving into the big leagues, I had started to take on a different set of responsibilities.

My little brother Butch wasn't doing so well at school.

In the fall of 1989, our middle brother Damon had just gone off to pursue a prestigious degree at Villanova University in Pennsylvania. With Damon out of the house, Roland long gone, and my mom working the same government job, no one was there to bolster Butch in his scholastic efforts. Mom and I could see the writing on the wall. He was hanging out with a lot of older guys, guys who weren't in school anymore. Fears that he would follow in Roland's footsteps hung heavy over my thoughts. When I told my mom that Butch could move in with me and that I would take on the responsibility of mentoring him, he had almost two years of high school left to finish.

It felt like a win-win. Butch and I got to spend a lot of one-on-one time together, which was wonderful for both of us. He needed a father figure, someone to give him real talk and life advice. I needed to feel like I had everything under control. I was still in a relationship with someone, but I wasn't going to let that get in the way of supporting my brother.

From what I could tell when he moved into my spare room, Butch was smart enough to graduate. He had just been distracted. I thought that he might have had some kind of attention deficit, or that he was just too busy being the social butterfly to concentrate on his classes. My place was safe, quiet, calm. And given that both of us knew that Damon was more academically talented than either of us, I thought Butch and I could bond over the practicalities of getting through an education as a means to an end. It might be the first and the last time that we'd be a brotherhood of two, without our intelligent, quieter middle sibling.

Butch and I got into a good groove. His job was going to school every day while I was at work, but we'd go grab dinner and play video games every single night. On the weekends, he would hang out with me and my girlfriend, and we'd go to the movies, shopping at the mall, or to an Orioles game. I noticed that he really didn't make any friends, but at the time it was a relief given that my mom had been concerned about his social crowd back home. It just felt good that he and I were so close, that he was cool hanging and spending time with me.

I didn't know something wasn't right until I came home one day, having forgotten something important for work, and he was home. It wasn't that Butch was doing anything terrible; he just wasn't at school. Wasn't dressed. Wasn't even out of bed, and it was the middle of the day.

I sat down on Butch's bed and listened.

"I just... I mean, I don't know. I don't know," he stated unemotionally.

"Yeah, but you're supposed to be doing what people expect you to do, Butch. You're supposed to be in school. All you had to do is show up. I wasn't asking you to get straight As, dude."

"I just don't wanna go. There's nothing for me to do there."

"There's nothing for you here! This is not gonna work out if you're not gonna go. This is a let-me-down moment. Like, I stepped up for you. I feel for you, and I'm trying to provide for and nurture you, and get you away from DC because I know there are people in that environment who don't have your back."

"I know," he said. He wasn't defiant. He just seemed checked out.

Before that moment, Butch and I were having a lot of fun and a really good vibe. Brothers hanging out. Fried chicken on the counter. Not cleaning up all the time. We could do whatever we wanted. And then when he wasn't going to school, it killed the spirit of togetherness that we had created. I didn't want to be the source of tension. I didn't want to lose my connection to my brother by holding his pencil down to his paper and forcing him to do his homework. I thought that the security that I gave him, the love I offered Butch, was going to be enough. It wasn't.

I had a parent-teacher meeting and found out that Butch had not missed just a day or two but most classes, most days.

Then I got my mom on the phone.

"He needs some constant, constant care, Mom. He cannot be left on his own because he's gonna disappoint. He tells people—he tells me, his teacher, his principal—that he's done his homework or that he needs just a little more time, and people believe him. He's convincing. But none of it is real. He's not even trying."

"I thought he'd be better with you," she said. "You thought he'd be better with you, didn't you? He's just bored; he's always been bored."

"Yeah, but Butch needs to understand that he has a responsibility to not be bored. School has things other than, you know, classes."

"He's not like you, Derek. You were always so on top of things. You were always the one I could count on."

"Mom, you could count on me because I had no choice. I had to get things done because Roland was not a real dad. He's still not around, not that I'd want Butch to lean on him right now because that would be even worse. We need a real solution. But I'm at work all day long, and I can't tie Butch to a desk."

"I know. Derek, it's not all on you."

"You've got to take Butch back home. You know this is too much for me to do on my own. At least you have your sisters around. We pulled together before; the grandparents helped. Couldn't someone else help? Isn't there some kind of plan we can make?"

There wasn't anyone else. There wasn't another plan.

I sent him back, and I knew I was sending him back into harm's way. I wrestled with it, the feeling of loss gnawing at me, knowing where Butch might land. Knowing Roland's legacy. Knowing that I was fighting my way clear of that legacy, and Damon was trying just as hard to get out, to get away. At that moment, Butch didn't have any fight left.

Butch went back to DC, and approximately six months later, I was promoted to a new job, so I did too.

WHEN EARL GRAVES called me over for a meeting at his home in Virginia sometime in early 1991, I was overwhelmed to see thirty Ralph Lauren suits laid out on a table.

Graves's ability to shake hands and press the flesh was remarkable. He was kissing babies everywhere he went. In his world, relationships mattered completely, from Wall Street to the hood. He wanted to establish relationships with people, wanted to help people, wanted to learn from people, wanted to connect people. Always well dressed and laser-sharp, he could pass time with blue-collar workers and light up the room as easily as he could connect with White Plains executives. He was a star.

There were thirty years' worth of three-piece suits in front of me from the '70s, '80s, and early '90s. There were a lot of bell-bottoms, but every suit was expertly tailored in the most expensive light wools, designed for East Coast weather.

"If they fit, you can take them home because my closet is overflowing," Graves said to me. "Of course you can have them altered. I don't wear these anymore. Take whatever ones that you want. And don't say no. Whatever ones you don't want will all be donated so you go try them on."

He ushered me into his bathroom like I was one of his kids running around in a department store. Remarkably, a lot of the clothes fit. The trousers needed some hemming because although I'm a tall man, he was taller, and there was some tapering needed to modernize the suits. I took every one of those suits home with me. I felt like I was literally stepping into a new version of myself, a version of Derek Lewis shaped by Earl Graves.

"So now at least I have a wardrobe," I remember saying to Sherene.

"Now there's a whole lot more you got to do in addition to putting a suit on. But that's a good start," she replied. "You command that attention. You command that respect. People want to hear from you. They want to know what you're talking about."

Moving back to DC was bittersweet for me. I had a big career opportunity in front of me and I got to do it in a place in which I was very familiar with the landscape, literally and figuratively. But I was going to miss Baltimore. I had a lot of fun living and working there. It was the first place I lived where I was truly on my own, and the first place where I got to make choices about how I lived. I was earning good money; I got to develop new, exciting relationships with people my age. Work was challenging and I was coping with Butch at home, but each night as I left work, I had the chance to decompress by playing hoops, going to sporting events, hanging out with frat brothers, or meeting up with other young Black professionals at local restaurants.

Even so, when the opportunity came about to work for Earl Graves, it was pretty hard to consider turning it down.

I still remember going up to New York on a train to interview with Graves at *Black Enterprise* headquarters. I was very nervous but excited about being on his team at Pepsi in DC. Graves wasn't carving out franchises; together with his new business partner Magic Johnson, they had a vision of working with influencers and businesspeople to make something special happen, treating their territory like a start-up and reconstructing the whole corporate operation around operations facilities.

"Mr. Graves, I want to drive significant growth in the District of Columbia because your name recognition, your value as a businessperson, means so much to this community," I remember saying in a flood of commitment to these powerful Black leaders. "And Magic, I'll show you that, as an athlete, you can really lift the Pepsi-Cola brand. I know this place. I know this community."

One of the reasons I joined Pepsi was that the Black management experience was front and center on their agenda, and Graves was a significant part of that. A lot changed after that. Graves set the stage for not only who I was to become but everyone at the company. Understanding diversity not only opened up more equity and equality for Pepsi employees, but it also had an immediate bottom-line impact.

"All of a sudden, Pepsi's market share became much more significant in many places. PepsiCo now understands the meaning of diversity," Graves explained a few years down the line in 2003. "The executives understand the difference it can make to market share. They understand the difference diversity can make in terms of image and community, and they understand that if they don't go after diverse markets, somebody else will. And so they think, 'Let's get on with this and let's become more serious about it.'"

And Graves was serious.

There was an infrastructure set up to accelerate Black leadership, and the white leadership believed in this plan. Black managers were provided support to be self-sufficient, to be very organized. Pepsi was, we were told, a great place for us to be to start our careers, build our careers, and finish our careers.

EARL GRAVES gave me the literal shirt off his back. It was a priceless act. I understand that he was wealthy enough not to care, but he did care. Although he didn't know it, he was doing me a solid at a time when I was as uneasy in my own skin as I would ever be as an adult.

Living up to our own expectations is not easy for any of us, especially at the beginning of our careers. Let me tell you a secret: that imposter syndrome does not go away. You may become the most experienced, talented, rich, or famous individual and you will still feel that gnawing personal doubt. That feeling doubles if you grow up in a disenfranchised community or home. I was handpicked by Graves and Magic to join their team. I was seen as strategic and creative in my field. I had the outer confidence to do my job well and feel that I had a strong-enough plan for the future. I knew Sherene loved me.

But I also knew that I had to keep on delivering at a high level if I wanted to ensure that I didn't fail, that my dream did not fade away. There was a part of me who was still the boy afraid of his own father, standing up to Joe, fronting with my 007 tag, my dark sunglasses, and my white Ford Escort.

Our training at Pepsi under Graves required a lot of role-playing. We played ourselves, and we were challenged to think critically about who we were and how we were coming across to others. When I was role-playing, I had to address some of the most fundamental issues that had come up in my journey to get to this point, this journey to being accepted as someone who could lead. My delivery probably wasn't always polished. I was probably a little rough, probably a little emotional at times, and my intensity was high. I may have been abrasive, but I was also being authentic.

Living up to our own expectations means setting aside those fears, not denying that they exist. Not pretending that you don't have emotions. Not shutting people out. It means asking for help, forging ever stronger relationships, offering solutions and connections so that you build a willing and able community of support around you.

I had tried to do the same for Butch as Graves had done for me. I was a willing and able support system for him. In many ways, I also failed him.

In the years since Butch lived with me, I've often thought about whether or not I could have supported him more fully, more as a father than as a brother. But my authentic self desperately craved brotherhood, and I had leaned into Butch's presence in the way I had leaned into being Kappa's dean of pledges. I missed the camaraderie of mentorship, of feeling connected with the men I inspired and who inspired me, especially in the days before cell phones and email. I wanted to be tight with Butch in the same way as I had mentored young Brothers at Hampton, but I didn't really grasp the fact that Butch needed more than that.

The culture that Graves created at Pepsi allowed me to be who I was. The Black Managers Association at Pepsi had the strategic horsepower to fast-track people like me and elevate us into new opportunities. Graves and Magic empowered Black managers to be very disciplined about articulating what their sales cohort needed. They pushed us to further development, further exposure, further growth to keep accelerating performance in their careers. As I built my sales practice, I was extremely motivated and driven, right out of the gate, to take off on this journey.

The more I was pushed, the more I thrived. The same was true for Damon. He walked a different path than me, but one where he could take his own lead.

But the more Butch was pushed, the more he pushed back against the constraints of expectations, of supposed-tos, of the life that our family wanted to have.

I felt like I was at the right place at the right time.

My little brother was not.

11

FAST EXIT

EVERAL DAYS after Christmas in 1994, I picked up the phone and my mother was frantic. Something was seriously wrong.

"I haven't heard from Butch."

"What do you mean? Like, since when?"

"He's been out for two straight nights. That's very unusual for him, Derek."

"You mean, he didn't even call to say he would be out? He's not answering his phone either? Hasn't even called today? Yeah, that's not normal."

It was two years after Sherene and I had gotten married. My career was moving along back in DC, and things were humming along. We had just landed in San Diego to visit her uncle to share the happy news that she was pregnant with our first child, so I wasn't able to just drive over to Mom's to support her that day.

"He normally would give me a heads-up if he wasn't planning to come home. But not to hear from him at all? Something is wrong. I know it."

"Maybe he's just with his friends and tied up," I said, trying to think of best-case scenarios to comfort my mom. "I'm sure he will be home tonight."

Another day went by, with no call, no show from Butch. Sherene and I both suspected that something was very wrong. Did he do something he regretted and was hiding out? Did something happen to him? I honestly wasn't sure what I wanted to believe to be true. In either case, I felt like we were all in a terrible position.

My mom ended up calling the morgue at DC General Hospital. They told her that they did not admit anyone with Butch's description in the time frame we shared, which provided some comfort in the moment. But the mystery of what happened and where Butch was holed up was still unsolved.

I was 2,600 miles away and I felt totally disconnected from not only my family but myself. San Diego was beautiful and all, but I just couldn't focus on what we were doing from day to day. Sherene and I did everything we could to try to take my mind off it. We went to SeaWorld and the San Diego Zoo and even drove up to the Forum in LA to see the Lakers and Pistons play. But I started to feel the impact of the stress and anxiety racing through my body. I was jittery and tired at the same time. Even watching some of the best in the world on the court, I couldn't concentrate on the game at all. All I could do is go over the situation back home in my mind, churning around the possibility that my brother was in harm's way. I spoke to my mom multiple times a day, and no news felt like terrible news. I kept praying that this would all work out. All I wanted was for Butch to be okay, and for our family to be back to normal.

Butch was twenty; I was twenty-seven. It was only a couple of years earlier that he had lived in my home. Not long after that, I had flown Damon and Butch down to Orlando with Sherene and me so that we could celebrate our engagement, spending time together at Disney World. We stayed in a time-share, going to the parks and hanging out at night and just having a real good time. Both of my brothers had been in my wedding party. I was still checking in on Butch, at least I thought I was.

The last time I had seen Butch was at Thanksgiving weekend, only a few weeks before Mom's call. Mom and I took him to a Washington Bullets game. We were cooking our favorite side dishes in the kitchen. It had been like old times, relaxing at Mom's, playing football on the PlayStation in the basement. Mom had recently purchased a house in a nice suburban Southern Maryland neighborhood, and I was happily going back and forth between her home and those of Sherene's relatives as we made the rounds as a newly growing family.

But under the surface, it was an uneasy time for all of us. Butch had just been let out from Prince George's County Correctional Center in Upper Marlboro, Maryland, for low-level dealing. It wasn't a prison, more of a facility where younger guys would get the scare put into them. Upper Marlboro was a suburban area close to DC, not too far from my own home or Mom's, where Butch was still officially living. He was locked up for six months, and I would drive over and see him in that facility, talking to him in front of the Plexiglas on the phone like we were characters on a television crime procedural.

When I had asked him what was going on, why he was suddenly working in the drug trade, I couldn't touch him. I couldn't reach him. Mom couldn't reach him. Neither could Damon, who had been his best friend growing up.

Butch was going to do what he wanted to do, no matter what anybody said to him.

In the last few years before his incarceration, Mom had tried to get Butch into a better school when he had moved back, but as Damon later told me, Butch beat people up in the hall; he was the bully in his class. I had tried to get Butch a job at Pepsi when he finally left school, but he didn't last long. It was much of the same—skipping out, cutting early. I had put my reputation on the line for Butch, but he didn't value what I valued. Later, Damon pulled some strings with a friend to get him a job at U-Haul, but Butch got in an accident that was serious enough to warrant an investigation. He tested positive for PCP and was fired.

Butch was impulsive and his focus was on getting money the fast way. He was smart, but he just decided to take short-cuts. Nothing stuck.

Even after losing job after job, at some point he got a vehicle. He started having money. And the strange thing is that he got along with everyone after that, especially Damon. As Damon says, the reality was that he was doing wrong, and everybody kind of turned a blind eye because he wasn't doing the kind of wild stuff anymore that we'd been able to clock in real time.

We just didn't know.

Thanksgiving had brought relief, however. The charges against Butch were suddenly dropped. He wasn't free to go on bail; he was free entirely. There wasn't going to be another court case, and he could just go home with Mom.

BACK IN SAN DIEGO, I couldn't think straight. For the first time in my life, I was experiencing anxiety attacks that felt like lead on my chest and light-headedness at the same time. I couldn't eat, and I was doing my best to socialize with

Sherene's close-knit family, a family that didn't know the kind of trauma I had borne throughout my childhood. I couldn't really explain the foreboding I felt, the sense that everything I knew, everything that really mattered back home in DC, was about to collapse.

The call came at five a.m. Sherene answered and handed me the phone immediately.

"He's gone. He's gone, he's gone, Derek."

"What? He's really gone? How? Why?"

My mom was screaming, sobbing. We finally found out what had happened, but the outcome of that interminable wait for information was the opposite of what we had hoped for.

Through her tears, my mom told us that police detectives had knocked on the door that morning. Butch had been shot and killed in southeast DC. He had seven bullet wounds in his torso. He had been lying in the morgue for a few days because of an identification mistake. Someone just didn't connect the dots. Even though Mom and Damon had called several times, the description they gave didn't get to the right people at the right time.

The news hit me harder than a ton of bricks. Butch was my younger brother. I loved him.

Sherene and I quickly changed our travel plans. Her uncle Clinton took us to the airport, and Sherene dealt with the ticket agent to get us on a plane back to DC as quickly as possible. I was sitting on the floor in the corner of the terminal crying, asking the same question of God over and over again: Why did this have to happen? We got on a plane in San Diego, connected in Houston, and were back in DC seven hours later.

WHEN WE started to put together the pieces, the act of violence perpetrated against my brother began to reveal its logic.

There was a reason that Butch had gotten out of the correctional facility. Mom had been angling for him to get out, negotiating with lawyers, but exiting his cell on a full release likely meant that Butch had begun to collaborate with law enforcement. We had been thrilled that he was coming home, but entirely naive as to why he was allowed to leave.

His body was found a short walk away from his car. Butch had likely taken a call to set up a meeting, or even a date with someone he already knew. In any case, we knew he felt he was safe because back at the car he had a weapon in the glove compartment. Butch didn't feel the need to have the gun on him.

Butch miscalculated.

Whatever he had revealed to the district attorney to get out of jail, it had reached someone. It could have been the simple fact that Butch had been released early that triggered that series of events, but we were told the chance that it was a retaliation hit was high. Butch didn't have the money or the power to get out of his predicament. He had the charm and charisma he was born with, but it wasn't enough. It was never enough.

Damon and I were hard on ourselves for months, for years, upset at the fact that we never were able to get Butch away from DC as soon as he was released. He was safer in corrections than he was outside. As Mom said, however, street justice takes care of itself. There was nothing Butch could do to run or hide. We did not know that there was a price on his head. Once you step into that life, you're tied to it.

For the rest of your life, there's just no way out.

He may not have ever realized it, but Butch got both the best and the worst of his traits from Roland. The impulsiveness, the gamesmanship, the deceitfulness. The constant drive to get quick hits. The charisma and quick wit. The shining bright ability to connect with people, to understand what he had to be in each living moment to get his needs met, was an intrinsic part of how he operated.

"I always thought he was living his life as if he knew he wasn't going to be around," Damon confided in me. "All of the stuff that we would deem to be super important—getting good grades, making a home for himself, finding a relationship— it didn't fit for him. He wasn't in his life for the long haul."

"I don't think it was intentional that he was going to get himself in trouble," I replied.

"No," Damon said. "In some ways, it was just a philosophical thing. It just wasn't a priority to do homework all night, for what? It's eerie to think that in his mind, he thought, 'I'm not gonna be here that long,' but I do think that he just knew. He didn't see himself being a long-term player."

Everything that Butch did had a very short window.

TRAUMA SHAPES us all differently.

The trauma of losing her son is embedded in my mother's heart. It cannot be unwoven from the trauma of her own teenage years and the abuse that she suffered as a wife. There is a part of me that believes that Mom wakes up every day and thinks about what happened that December. I believe that she returns to that moment every single day and is angry about how it happened and who did it and why it happened. She constantly reminds herself of that very traumatic situation, and in doing so she is actively doing trauma to herself every day.

Butch was living on borrowed time from childhood because of his own trauma. As the youngest child, he had the kind of support that I did not have, that Damon did not have. He was not coddled, but he did not have to eke his way through life, working and doing the heavy lifting I had to do. But perhaps even more important to Butch's story is the fact that he may have been, unbeknownst to Mom, physically affected by Roland's increasing drug use at his conception. This is something that science now knows is intrinsically connected to the ADHD and dopamine-deprivation symptoms that Butch was treated for when he was a child. I didn't know until much later in life that Butch had been medicated with Ritalin for several years because of his inability to concentrate.

Butch was also living on borrowed time because, like many Black men, research shows, Butch's cause of death was expected. In DC in the last several decades, the homicide rate is highest among Black men aged twenty to twenty-four years; it's the highest homicide rate of any racial or ethnic group. The most common cause of death is a gunshot wound. When the relationship between a homicide victim and a suspect was known, the suspect was most frequently an acquaintance or friend for male victims, just like Butch.

For both Damon and me, Butch's death had a significant pull on our life choices, and how we would interact with and support our immediate families.

We know that the legacy of our family is going to continue but that we have to take all necessary steps to maintain and embrace that legacy.

Damon and I make sure that our families are grounded in values of care, respect, and an obligation to pay our opportunities forward. We deliberately try to do good by people. We work hard. We place a priority on education for our children. The rewards are not as glamorous as those Butch was seeking, especially early on in life, but they can be as time goes on.

In a broken home, your odds are just different. So much of your ability to thrive is circumstantial. The fact that Damon and I have survived when Butch did not is a miracle. If things were flipped, I would have been in the same situation as Butch.

It wasn't luck. It wasn't planned. It wasn't forced by anybody. It just happened that way. I thank God for my ability to still live and work and try, but it could just as easily have been me pierced by those bullets.

I want Butch's story to be told and understood because there are too many families experiencing the same things as we did.

Everything is a struggle.

Everything is a fight.

Everything is overwhelming, and often life offers tragic circumstances.

Because I lived, I knew I had a responsibility to fight for Black families, to hold them in their struggle, to be a voice for caring and caregiving. Because of Butch, I knew that I wanted to offer up my support, to make it possible for young men to see that they can take any path that they want to take out of the suffocating fear of family violence.

We do not have to be the homicide victims that many of us seem fated to be. Like my mom showed me, there is a way forward by taking a government job and keeping your head down. Like my brother Damon showed me, there is a way forward through educating yourself and believing that you have the knowledge you need to make hard choices easier. Like I showed myself, there is a way forward through building your results, relationships, and reputation, slowly and carefully making yourself trusted by trusting you'll get there, eventually.

If you want to have the greatest possible chance of success, and give your children that chance, you have to be deeply involved in your family life. Your job has to involve reinforcing, every day, what good is, what responsibility is, what love is, what care is, what development is. Enter into a true partnership with your spouse or partner. Share principles of who you need to be for each other, and how you want to operate as a couple and as a family. Work together to develop building blocks and skill sets that will lead to the successes that you and your children *can* have.

There is a way forward.

There is a way through to the other side of a broken home.

That way to your own future? It has to come from within you, from that place inside where you know that you deserve better than what you were dealt.

12

REPUTATION

TWO MONTHS after Butch's passing, I was promoted to a new job in southern Ohio.

Leaving my mom and Damon so soon after Butch's death was bittersweet. I wanted to stay, but I didn't. I also felt the pull of escape. It would no longer be possible for me to just drive to Mom's and jump in to save the day.

PepsiCo owned several high-profile restaurant brands during the 1990s, namely Taco Bell, Pizza Hut, and KFC. At the same time, the company was aggressively promoting what it called SharePower, which was a stock option program. The goal was to drive long-term success for the entire organization by providing associates with incentives so that we'd take a greater level of ownership over PepsiCo operations. I was intrigued by this opportunity, so much so that I started to envision a future for myself where I'd work for every division of PepsiCo. As a result, I took an offer to dive into a market manager position at Taco Bell in Cincinnati. I wanted to expand my skills in a wholly different consumer engagement environment: quick service restaurants (QSRs).

Cincinnati was my chance to build a reputation as the enterprise go-to guy. I also wanted to get an MBA. I was going to do everything simultaneously: new job, new school, and soon taking on a new role in my family. I wanted it all. I wanted to be the game changer. I had a mission, and I had energy to burn.

In Cincinnati, everything started out well. I was lucky to have a tremendous boss, Tom Davin. Tom's region was South Central, stretching from Louisiana up to Ohio and down to the Florida panhandle. Not only did he have a top-notch business education, but he had served in the military. He was very sharp, very polished, very strategic, very disciplined, and had very strong people skills. There's something about a lot of people who emerge from the military that goes unnoticed: because they understand trauma, they can be very kind and patient. Tom expected me to move the needle quickly, but he also nurtured me. Because of Sherene's pregnancy and the fact that she had also been working for Taco Bell since she'd graduated from Hampton, I was allowed to do my six weeks of crew training close to home before we left, so that we could optimize our move logistics.

So that I could immerse myself in the work, I trained in a northern Virginia store, taking part in the same kind of shift work that any frontline QSR employee would have to show up for every single day.

The first day, I remember being handed a very thick manual called the "Answer Book" that detailed every operational procedure necessary to run an effective shift. It had the answers, but I had to do the work: washing dishes, emptying trash, restocking food, and keeping the dining room area tidy were all a part of my initial deep dive into Taco Bell. Later, I learned how to make food items and take orders from customers.

But the real learning curve was connected to the pure speed of QSR work.

Peak hours at lunch and dinner were very intense. Stacks of cars piled up in the drive-through lane while the inside lineups made it all the way to the store's front door. Late night was a whole different animal. Tacos, burritos, and other snack items flew off the production line. Watching the crew handling hundreds of transactions during these peak hours, I was impressed. Speed and accuracy meant everything. If we didn't get it right, if a guest was dissatisfied, we'd hear about it through Taco Bell's 1-800 number complaint line.

I loved every minute of my initial training experience. I had to evolve from training as a crew member to becoming a shift manager within four weeks. Every single role was one I knew intimately. By the end of my training, I truly understood not only the average Taco Bell customer but the pressure, tedium, and repetitiveness of working in a QSR.

Once I finished what amounted to Taco Bell boot camp, I began my general management training for the company in Louisville, Kentucky.

And then I was placed in one of the most challenging markets not only in the region but in the country. I was given the task of overseeing twenty-plus restaurants in southern Ohio and northern Kentucky.

The day-to-day (and night-to-night) experience in a fast-food restaurant was entirely different from any role I had experienced at Pepsi. This included the workforce.

At Pepsi, frontline employee tenure is expected. For most roles, employees are given the opportunity to advance into bigger or differentiated management roles as they acquire new skills. This leads to greater organizational stability, consistency, and performance. These jobs can be high pressure, but they are also very high reward.

Working in fast food, most of the frontline workers make minimum wage. They have limited opportunities to move up the corporate ladder. They might be in their first or their very last job. Most are not on a management track. For them, Taco Bell was just a way to pay the bills. It's a frontline culture, and it's hard work. Very hard work.

Added to this was the fact that the guests we served at Taco Bell were sometimes not the friendliest they could be. People can often be rude, they can yell at employees for no reason, and when late night comes, it can just get downright unruly at the drive-through. If you're ordering tacos at three a.m., you're not coming from church.

The conditions for success can be really challenging, especially if key ingredients are missing. I'm not talking about mild or hot sauce, but leadership, teamwork, training, and a solid work culture.

As soon as I showed up in my new market, I found the ideal place to start changing the status quo.

In training stores, conditions should be more ideal than most. You're meant to see what running a tight ship looks like in real time so that you can emulate it.

In the field, you understand why you've been brought in to help, and quickly.

On one of my very first store visits in the new role, I arrived during a lunch rush and quickly noticed that we had a bottleneck on the line producing food. Wait times were escalating, and customers were becoming frustrated. My first instinct was to ensure all hands were on deck (we called this "aces in place"). I could tell we didn't have many experienced team members on the shift, so I pulled the assistant manager aside to make some decisions before jumping in on the line to help eliminate the bottleneck. If we could stem the tide for the next sixty minutes, I thought, we could recover and get ready for the next peak. I was on the steam station, warming the tortillas and adding meat or beans, handing off my orders to the "stuffer" who was filling in lettuce, cheese, and other add-ons and wrapping the final product. When I went to grab my first tortilla, I noticed the date on the package: the tortillas had already expired. Becoming a little more frustrated at this point, I had to think on my feet quickly. Food safety had to be our first priority, so I checked the other ingredients to ensure we didn't have the same problem. Fortunately, I had caught the only expired package just in time.

We were lucky, but I was also relieved that my training had kicked in exactly when I needed it. We rebounded and finished the lunch hour on a high note. We huddled right after the shift to debrief our experience so that dinner and late night would run smoother. I listened carefully as all team members weighed in on what had to improve and what resources we needed.

This wasn't a lost cause, I thought. We could be great at this customer service thing if we took the time to communicate, plan, and execute together. What was necessary was a solid leadership effort from the managers every shift, every day, no matter what.

In Louisville during my final training weekend, I experienced a perfect QSR storm. The morning started out great. We opened on time. I took last night's deposit to the bank. The weather was forecasted to be great. We were fully staffed and set up.

All of a sudden, things took a very sharp turn. The computer system broke down on the lunch rush. We had to input the orders manually, and I was making drinks while talking to some IT person on Taco Bell's 1-800 line to get us back up and running. We were giving it our all, hustling, being courteous, supporting one another. While our order processing speed times were low, we were having fun dealing with the adversity. Despite the chaos, there was a sense of calmness that came over the team during that peak rush that was super impressive.

"We're going be just fine the rest of the day," I was thinking as I rebooted the POS systems.

All of a sudden, I heard a loud scream from the customer service area. I turned around, and a woman had fallen onto the floor, her face blue. Her daughter was in a panic, and she was clearly in physical distress. I dropped the 1-800 call and called 911, and immediately shut down the store. We were in luck because an ambulance arrived in minutes, and they pulled the woman into the ambulance and took off.

"Are you okay?" I said to the daughter, who was gathering her mother's things to take to the hospital. "Give me your number. We're going to be praying for you, so please let us know what happens."

"It didn't look good. I'm sorry," she said, starting to cry.

"I'm sorry too," I said.

Two hours later, she did call me back. Her mother had died in the hospital.

I was shell-shocked and saddened. The rest of the afternoon was a blur. I had to call corporate to tell them what had happened. Media outlets were calling the store asking for a statement, so I had to call the PR department in California to manage the situation. The Taco Bell communications team wanted to know what the customer had eaten, but neither of the women had received their order when the emergency took place. We reopened shortly thereafter, reassuring guests there were no food safety issues.

It felt like everything was moving at a hundred miles an hour. The crew stayed strong, but within a short period of time, I was dealing with a shift change and a big truck order out back that needed to be transferred to the cold box. I had to gather myself to deal with the realities of what needed to be done so we could set up the night team for success.

But the hits kept coming.

It was five thirty p.m. and I was about to leave when the closing shift manager called out sick. With only three crew members on the docket until our planned four a.m. close, I had to perform a double: two back-to-back ten-hour shifts. It wasn't only going to be physically difficult but mentally taxing. Finding my second wind, we ended up having a great shift. But because of all the events that had occurred earlier in the day, closing the store and the books was going to take much longer than normal. Policy stated that no one could be at the store by themselves, and I was very appreciative of the crew member who offered to stay with me. Fatigued, I made multiple mistakes and had to repeat my tasks until I finally locked the doors at seven thirty a.m., a twenty-four-hour workday.

Once I left the restaurant, I went straight to Cracker Barrel to celebrate.

"After that, I'm ready for anything," I said to myself. "Here we come, Cincinnati!"

I HAD TO BE READY for more than anything, as I found out quickly.

I already had the playbook in my mind when I came in the door, but one night, Sherene's commitment made all the difference to me. At the time, she was still living in DC until she went on maternity leave, but we were both flying out to be with each other on alternate weekends.

One weekend, she got off the plane on a Friday and called me at the restaurant at ten p.m.

"When are you going to be back at the hotel?"

"I'm not," I said. "Everyone's called out sick, and there's only three of us here now, and one of my team has to leave at midnight to take care of his kids."

"Okay, I'll just come down the restaurant."

"What do you mean?"

"I mean I'm coming to Taco Bell, Derek."

She basically took over, pregnant and in there working on the line. Sherene had much more QSR experience than I did. I took the drive-through headset because I had the patter. She was on the line making the food, because she was great at it. The last crew member ran customer service. We turned the music up and we stayed till four in the morning. It was crazy, but we had a lot of fun, and looking at her stepping right in to help made me feel better, whole, supported, and equipped to lead when I had to roll in at eight a.m. the next day.

Taco Bell should be fun. All work should be fun. In Cincinnati, I turned things around not by punishing workers and making them push harder. I turned things around by making sure that every shift in every store had managerial coverage. I wanted to make sure that all of our frontline customer service folks could rely on a higher-level manager. There was a crew member running the ship every day who had the experience and know-how to support and to lead, and to pick up the slack just like Sherene had volunteered to do in my time of need.

Doing things my way meant more promotions, more incentives, and more money spent on human resources.

Now, the holistic actions I introduced in Cincinnati were not in the managerial handbook I received when I was hired. My recommendations went against the grain. But my ideas showed my higher-ups that over-betting on people and culture would result in better revenue, profit, customer service performance, and higher financial payouts for managers. That's why I was able to push through the changes that I wanted. The changes did wonders for retention and morale across all positions. We were on a mission to not to just get by but to create a best-in-class environment where everybody wins. I taught people to act like owners. I empowered them. I provided the right resources. Everyone felt like they were part of a team that was very connected and focused on the same goals.

Within one year, Cincinnati became a top ten market for Taco Bell.

13

ROLAND

GETTING A CALL from my mom underlined everything that I was learning about starting my own family with Sherene, for better or for worse.

"Derek, I'm at the hospital. Roland is in bad shape."

"What happened, Mom? What's wrong with him?" I asked.

"The doctors need to talk to you since I'm not his next of kin," she admitted. "So I don't know exactly, but I know it's not good."

I had not spoken to my father in nearly two years. In fact, the last time I spoke with him was the day before Butch's funeral. I had called Roland to confirm the time our limo was going to pick him up on the way to the church.

"Eight a.m.," I had said. "We'll see you then."

I called again the morning of the funeral to let him know we were on our way. Roland never picked up. He never showed up either. My father did not say goodbye to his son.

That had been the final straw for me. I didn't care if I ever saw or spoke to him again. If that was the way it was going to be, so be it.

Now, two years after my brother's death, my father was struggling to hang on, breathing in his final hours on Earth.

"Let me check flights to see when I can get to town," I said to my mom.

"Okay," she replied. "But I don't think there's much time left."

I got off the phone with Mom and dialed the number I had jotted down on a piece of paper. The doctor told me that my father had experienced septic shock and pneumonia.

"He's in bad shape. We've had to resuscitate him once, and he was stable. But he's not stable now, meaning that we've got him hooked up but he's not breathing on his own. It's not a good situation. When can you come to town?"

I thanked him and booked a flight. Even considering all of the possible routes from Cincinnati to DC, the absolute earliest I could get to town was the next morning, and I let Mom know.

I prayed that Roland would make it through the night. It felt like this was the end for him. My emotions were mixed. I looked at this moment as a final chance to reconcile things with him face-to-face before it was over. I was feeling some guilt, feeling as if I had given up on him. He was my father, and he was a human being. People make mistakes, right? I found some solace in thinking that now Roland could finally reunite with my brother and begin to make up for lost time.

Around midnight, I got another call.

"We're resuscitating him every fifteen minutes now," the doctor said. "What do you want us to do? Do you want us to keep going until you get here?"

"Let him go peacefully," I said. "Make it peaceful. But just let him go."

Two hours later, Roland was gone.

I still got on the plane the next day because someone had to plan and pay for a funeral. No one else was going to do it.

A funeral for a family like Roland's was never going to be easy.

Roland had a huge extended family, and most of his siblings lived in New Jersey. I knew all my aunts and uncles but hadn't seen them in a while. My mom had kept them in the loop on his condition and his passing. With help from my mom and brother, I took care of all the details. Damon read scriptures, and I wrote and presented the eulogy.

The funeral was held on Thursday, September 5, 1996, in Forestville, Maryland, a year and a half after we laid Butch to rest. It was a really good service. It was short and sweet, but intimate and heartfelt. Many of Roland's siblings showed up, which was very comforting.

The funeral brought closure for me in many ways, or at least I thought it did. At the end of the service, just as I finished thanking everyone for coming and walked down from the podium, a man I didn't know walked up to me.

"Hi, my name is Morty. I'm your brother. Daddy and I were just talking about you not so long ago."

All of a sudden, there's someone new claiming to be my half brother. Knowing Roland, it didn't surprise me. I just stood there, silent. Roland's casket was still in plain sight. I was just about to help the other pallbearers move it into the hearse; I was watching it out of the corner of my eye.

"So you want to talk about the house?" he asked.

"Respectfully, I don't know who you are," I replied, "and this is certainly not the time to be having this conversation. Let's pick this up at another time."

Knowing Roland, if he was indeed his father, Morty's request didn't surprise me either. I got his number and walked away.

EVENTUALLY, MORTY AND I had a conversation. He didn't want to connect. He didn't want to build a relationship. He was solely interested in claiming a stake in the house that my dad had been living in when he passed away. The house wasn't worth very much at all. It was small and insignificant in financial terms. Even though it wasn't a big deal, it felt like a burden. I couldn't believe I was even dealing with this with everything I had going on.

But the situation had to be dealt with. I hired a lawyer, and she told us that the only way we were going to figure this out would be to have a DNA test, and that legally we'd have to exhume Roland's body to do it. She didn't think it was worth doing, given the value of the house. By the time we'd pay for the exhumation, it would be very little to spread around, win or lose.

"Well, I guess we'll just split it," I said to the lawyer. "You know, if I can't prove it, I don't want this to go any further. I don't want to keep this going on forever."

Magically, a day later the lawyer called me back.

"I got great news."

"What happened?"

"Morty was legally adopted by another family years ago. He can't claim Roland's estate."

Damon and I ended up selling the house and splitting the proceeds evenly, and I got a check that helped pay a couple of bills.

MANY BLACK FAMILIES are connected by secrets and complexity. We were separated as chattel, as property, never to see each other again. Mother from child, wife from husband, sibling from sibling. We are part of a hidden system of people who were never permitted to claim each other, to be families, to act as one.

How large is my family? I actually have no idea. We never found out whether Morty was a match to Roland's DNA, but it's possible. I could have more siblings out there. In some ways I feel like this pattern of connection and disconnection may be the norm for Black families in a lot of places.

I was not on a quest to find out everything about my family's past. Even in the present day, I have accepted that my family is what it is. But at that moment, just as I moved into fatherhood, into becoming Team Lewis with Sherene, my father's death and who he represented to me became meaningful.

Why me, now?

How did I get here?

Losing Butch. Finding out about my sister. Losing Roland. Gaining Morty, even for a few days. Knowing that I didn't really know the full story. As much as I searched for the pieces of the puzzle, I knew that there would always be a few missing.

All of it made me question the person I was and the choices I had made. As much as I had made the effort to become the man I wanted to be, to mentor myself and others, I felt that there was a part of me that might fail. That part of me was tied to the father I had but never really was able to call my own.

I wanted never to be like Roland. He was never a real dad to me or my brothers. I only called him by his first name. He was a part of me, but he also was alien to me.

I wanted to protect my children from this alienation, this longing for connection and closeness, this distrust of a father that I had always borne.

I wanted more than that for them. And so I had to make it happen.

14

GOOD SPORTS

SOON AFTER we set up our new Ohio home, Sherene became a mother, and I became a father for the first time. Our first son was born, and we named him Devon. We named our son in honor of Butch, using his real name, his birth name.

It was a time of massive transition. So, because we wanted Devon's birth to feel safe and secure and welcoming, we planned to be back home at Sherene's parents' home in Maryland. She gave birth at Shady Grove Adventist Hospital with the gynecologist she had trusted to manage her pregnancy. We had a warm, comforting place to stay for a couple of weeks with family before we had to get back into high gear.

It was time for me to step up, to embody everything I had been planning for up until this moment.

"It's your turn now," I said to myself, sitting there during the labor and waiting, contemplating everything that would come next. "This is your moment. Don't blow it. Everything that you felt about your dad and the lack of that bond, the lack of that ownership, the lack of that support network, remember it. Remember all of that. You get to be on the other side of it. Embrace this. This is what you wanted."

It was a talk I gave to myself, but one that was so important. I took every advantage of being a father.

I remember the first time Sherene had to go on a work trip. Neither of us had to travel very often while we were living in Ohio, but it happened the week she was away there was a contest at a local mall calling for children to come and get their photos taken. Like any young couple, we were excited about dressing up our beautiful boy and taking him out. Sherene had left me with instructions along with a perfectly coordinated tiny outfit for Devon to wear. Make sure you get him dressed nicely, brush his hair, be there on time. It was a wonderful time for us, I thought as I got him ready to go, all done up for the camera. He and I were looking our best, and Devon even ended up winning the photo contest. He was the most photogenic and well-behaved kid, and we still have that picture hanging in our home today.

He got a lot of love and nurturing from us and from his grandparents. My whole life was about being a great dad. I wanted to take care of him.

I also wanted to take care of Sherene. I think being a great dad helps you become a better spouse. Nurturing your children is a key component of your family life, and so if you see your partner doing all the right things, you're going to feel good about that. The same goes for when your spouse is struggling. Holding each other up is critical, so that you can do your best every day. When both spouses are supported, your children have the best you have to offer.

That's why we became Team Lewis.

What was good for each of us was good for all of us.

THE MOMENT Devon was born was the moment I had been waiting for all of my life.

It was the moment I became everything.

I wanted a great career. I wanted a wonderful wife and partner. I wanted a house to call my own. But the thing that I was most looking forward to was being a dad.

Devon came into the world at a very difficult time because I had just lost my brother, someone whom I had, in many ways, fathered. I didn't want to forget about him. It's why Sherene and I made the solemn decision to name our first son after his uncle. I knew doing so would help me continue to remember my brother every time I saw my son. Saying his name allowed me to connect to my brother.

Sherene had spent the last weeks of her pregnancy back with her parents. It just made sense. She trusted her Maryland ob-gyn team, and we had only just relocated to Ohio. Having Sherene's mother around when she gave birth was important as well. There would be time enough to get him back to Ohio and start our family life together.

But in those last few weeks, all I could think about was what was going to happen next. It was a pivotal time for me, a time when I was able to reset many wrongs, many losses, all at once. Devon's birth meant a tremendous amount of new responsibility for me. I was okay with that. I wanted that. I didn't want to run from it.

At the same time, we ended up stacking all these extra cards one on top of the next: a new baby in a new city with a new job. And because it was early in her career, Sherene had to get back to work sooner rather than later. We needed to make sure we didn't fail.

Luckily, we were able to create a support system that worked.

One of my fraternity brothers connected us with his older auntie, Laura, whom we hired as our daycare and general household support. We had to get over that hurdle of trusting somebody with our three-month-old son, but she was fantastic. Having a mature and experienced woman on our team meant that every time I picked Devon up, he was happy.

Sherene and I played tag team with Devon, depending on our rapidly changing schedules. Even though we were both working fairly long hours during the week, weekends were when we hunkered down as a family. We were happy on the weekend, just hanging out. The three of us would go to family restaurants, Devon right there with us in his little high chair. We even took him to games once he was a year old, bundling him up in a blanket in the cold weather. Wherever we went, Devon was there.

I was very intentional about fatherhood. It was an opportunity to be the man I wanted to be, perhaps for the first time in my life. I was no longer just trying to fit together the pieces of my life. Everything I needed to puzzle out was done. I was a husband and father, and putting my all into each role made me better at both.

Without a paternal role model, I had to make things up on the fly. In my childhood household, I often felt like I was walking on eggshells. Sometimes I would come home just hoping people were not in a bad mood. I wanted to stay outside. I didn't want to go back in the house. I didn't want to deal with the drama, the uncertainty of the environment, the possibility that a heavy object would be flying across the room during a fight.

But if I was going to become a leader in a household, I was going to do things differently.

We were all going to become good sports.

SPORTS ARE more than games.

In the beginning of my parenting life, all I knew was that I loved participating in sports, whether as a player or as someone cheering on my favorite teams. Sports was something that Sherene and I shared as well. So, just as football season tickets defined our family outings in the early days, we continued to lean in to sports as a recreational activity.

But as I began to parent for real as Devon started to walk, talk, and then run, I recognized that sports had an even bigger role to play in our family.

Sports was already a constant, but what if it could be a teaching tool, a bonding tool, and a tool for life?

As a family, we leaned into team sports heavily, rather than individual athletics. Team sports had everything I was looking for when it came to setting a path forward for Devon and then Jordan and Kellan.

Lesson one: sports require routine.

I didn't want to be the kind of dad who would grind his kids every day: "Make your bed. Clean your room. Go clean up the yard." That wasn't the way I wanted to deal with them. I wanted them to learn the value of routine so that they would be self-interested in making their own lives better, bit by bit. I didn't want them to sweat the small stuff; I wanted them to take care of it as a matter of course and not complain. Playing sports puts a lot of value on the kind of muscle memory that can only be achieved through practice. Soon, what was once hard becomes rote, and then the game becomes that much more exciting.

Lesson two: sports have high highs and low lows, but you still keep playing.

Most sports teams are going to experience wins and losses, ups and downs, all season long. Sure, it's great to be on a winning team, but for kids it's also important to learn how to lose. I wanted my kids to experience both so that they could gain the kind of equanimity and calm that they'd need to ride the roller coaster that is life. Sports requires competition, but more than anything it requires you to compete with yourself. Getting to that personal best is what matters most.

Lesson three: getting access to coaching is like adding another parent into the mix.

When my kids started playing sports, I had a sudden realization that they were bringing home as many lessons as I was teaching them. Why? Because they had coaches. If they were playing more than one sport in a school year, they might have access to two or even three coaches who volunteered or were paid to guide them and cheer them on. For any kid, that coaching relationship can be special. It's a chance to get another opinion on what you are doing right and what you might do better. And different coaches come into play throughout a child's sporting life. Interacting with every one of these dedicated people allowed for significant positive shifts in the way that Devon, Jordan, and Kellan saw themselves in the world.

Finally, lesson four: team sports put you under pressure to come through for other people.

When you're on a team, you know that what's at stake is that everyone is counting on you. Sure, if you're having a bad day, someone else can pick up the slack. But if you let your team down, the person who will feel that loss the most is yourself. On a sports team or on Team Lewis, I taught my kids that being a good person is a foundation for getting things done and coming through in the end.

I chose a sports metaphor for parenting because it worked, but I also chose sports because that's what I wanted. It was important for me to set my own standard for what mattered within my family. As a parent, I wasn't just undoing old patterns embedded in me by my family experiences, I wanted more. I wanted it to feel good. I wanted to act as a catalyst for making my kids' lives extraordinary, so that they could become who they wanted to really be.

Sports made their lives easier because, on the surface, my kids *were* playing games. They learned their life lessons the easy way, at least a much easier way than I had learned the same rules for life.

Sometimes, in the moment, these lessons were still very difficult for my children. There were times when I put them through their paces.

"Why are you yelling at me for losing a basketball game, Dad?" I remember Devon asking me one evening as we were driving home.

"I'm not yelling because you lost. I'm raising this issue with you because I didn't see the effort from you. Your effort wasn't high-level enough for that loss. You let your team down, and you let yourself down and you could do better. Imagine if you set the example for putting in the effort, what that would do to help the team."

"Yeah, okay," he said.

"It doesn't matter what position you play either. Your role is to set the example and do what you have to do to play at your best each and every game. Sometimes you're going to win, sometimes not. But it's more about the process. You can prepare yourself in ways that allow you to execute your talent at the highest level you possibly could. Right?"

"Yeah, Dad. I get it."

"You're going to run into more superior talent, you're gonna run into more superior coaching, whatever it may be. But that should not stop you from being your best."

LIKE ME, my kids weren't raised in an entitled home. Although I eventually became very successful in my career, we were a middle-class family for the majority of their childhood, working hard to get where we are today. But together, Sherene, Devon, Jordan, Kellan, and I made our own dreams come true.

I saw the potential in them to be great athletes and to play sports perhaps even on a professional level, as Jordan has gone on to do. All of my kids have been Division 1 athletes. But even more so, the lessons we learned together had a positive impact on my children, on me, and on all of us as a family.

Right now, I know that all of my children have far exceeded my expectations in terms of their personal development and maturity. The process was not just about getting trophies or hanging up a certificate. Although putting the kids into a sports mindset was a way of living out my own dream, they set their own bars higher than I imagined.

My job as a father, together with Sherene as their mother, was to create the environment in which anything was possible.

To help all three kids see their potential, even if their future wasn't about sports.

To ensure that our children believed in themselves.

To generate excitement about achievement, eking out that next point, that next win, and building on a foundation of practice and commitment.

To have quiet confidence in making choices for themselves.

To create the impetus for their performance, leveraging it in the best way possible for their future happiness.

Parenting, for me, emerged from a fantasy to become a dream come true.

15

SCRAMBLE

ON THE WESTERN SHORES of the North Sea, the world seems practically still despite the winds drafting inland and the sound of the gulls. It is an old place, a calm one, a land shaped by the crashing of waves so that sand pools as naturally as the tides. The water laps through funnels in the green coastal grasses, and the sun hits low. It's far away from urban centers, home to a castle on a hillside, its ramparts peacefully crumbling in the sun. And it's home to one of the best damn golf courses in the history of sport.

St Andrew's is a private members' golf club with access to seven different courses, the most hallowed ground in the world of golf. Having opened in 1843, the club is one of the oldest by far and likely the most vaunted, for good reason.

My MBA team had to be in London ready to work at eight a.m. Monday morning, but I had just landed in Scotland via the red-eye from Cincinnati to Heathrow. It was my first trip to Europe, and there was no time to lose when I got off the plane.

Four of us grabbed our bags and got into a rental car. We had a ninety-minute drive northeast of Edinburgh ahead of us, and every minute counted, because for the next thirty-six hours or so, the greens at St Andrew's would be our playground.

The year I got to St Andrew's, 1997, was the year that Tiger Woods won three PGA Tour events as well as the Masters and ranked number one in the world golf ranking for the first time in his life. That year was the first that anyone had seen a Black man as the global leader in golf. He was on fire, dominating his field for 264 consecutive weeks until 2004. Tiger had been playing the game since he was a toddler in Orange County, California, making his national TV debut on *The Mike Douglas Show* at two years old, joined by his father, Earl, and legendary comedian Bob Hope.

I was no Tiger Woods. Tiger was only twenty-one years old when he was lauded as the greatest athlete of his generation, and I was twenty-three years old when I was first introduced to golf.

At Pepsi, we sponsored and played in numerous customer charity golf events throughout the season. So, when one of the first tournaments of the year came up in 1990, I got in touch with my grandfather. At the age of seventy, he was on the green on a regular basis in DC. He hadn't been playing that long. In fact, he didn't take up the game until he retired. I wanted to be prepared for our foursome, and I asked him what kind of equipment I needed. I went over to Sports Authority to buy a set of clubs, balls, a glove, and some new shoes.

I had never swung a golf club before. I took my grandfather's advice and went to a local driving range and attempted to practice. I had some good shots and lots of bad shots. What I discovered was that I really loved swinging that club.

The day of the tournament, I had to tell myself not to put any pressure on this outing.

"Just go with the flow," I said to myself. "Watch, learn, socialize, and, most importantly, have fun. It's golf. It's meant to be relaxing."

I was playing in a scramble format. It's a game where the team selects the best shot from the four players' efforts. Everyone plays their next shot from that chosen spot. This continues throughout the entire round. In a scramble, you don't have to try to be a hero on every shot. A scramble makes the round both faster and more fun. It's all about collaboration. That day, the team had my back, and I had their back. We worked together, we supported each other, we laughed at how bad some of our shots were, and we cheered loudly when someone hit a great one. The overall tournament was a huge success.

After the customer outing, I made it a point to start playing regularly. So at least one or two times a week, my grandfather and I would play or meet at the driving range to hit balls together.

My grandfather, Perry we called him, was a workaholic and a provider, a quiet authority figure in our family. He was consistent. He did not disappoint anyone. It helped that when we were on the links, we started having more conversations about life and business and what I wanted to do to shape my future. Golf shifted our formerly transactional relationship into something deeper. It felt like we both had the opportunity to begin to rewrite some of our history and the father-son challenges that I had experienced at home.

Soon I was playing golf with my fraternity brothers on Saturday and then with my wife, grandfather, and Uncle Gary on Sunday. During the weekdays after work during the summer, I'd go to driving ranges or visit a local golf center to look at the latest and greatest equipment. I needed to get an edge when I played with the other guys. It helped that Sherene played the game as well. We rotated when and where we'd play, spend the whole day together, and then go to dinner or a movie. I had discovered a joy in playing golf that I did not expect, that I didn't see coming.

Golf taught me how to be more strategic.

I WAS IN EUROPE because it wasn't enough for me to take on a new job in the QSR industry and welcome my first child into the world, all in the same year. I decided it was time to get my MBA, and I was going to pursue an executive MBA at Xavier University in Ohio at the same time as well. It had an excellent executive MBA program that wasn't easy to get into. I was determined to get in the program beginning in the fall of 1996. There was no stopping me.

Life felt urgent, as if it had to be lived, as if I had to do everything I could do and more, all at once. Once my son Devon had arrived, it was all I could do to be the father I never had. I needed to be dependable but flexible. Loving but someone who would hold my children to high enough expectations. Financially stable but not indulgent. Available but also producing the kind of on-the-job results that would ensure my children would never be at risk.

All of that meant that I had to keep eking my way up. My career couldn't become stagnant, or I'd be letting myself and Sherene down. Once I had been inside corporate America for a couple of years, I realized that your profile was expanded and enhanced if you had an advanced degree. People with MBAs got tagged differently, and when I started to move up the ranks, I was competing with people who had advanced degrees. Before we moved to Ohio, I had tried my hand at a traditional MBA at the University of Maryland, but things were just too complicated. Given my work schedule, I had been taking two classes, four days a week, getting home at ten o'clock at night or later most school nights. Weekends were filled with homework and studying for exams. I missed most study group sessions because they were during the day when I was at work. I was discouraged by how long the process would be: three years just to get through my coursework. Everyone in the classroom seemed to be a lot younger and less experienced than me.

At Xavier, the whole program was paced differently, in a way that perfectly aligned with my schedule and those of other management- and C-suite-level classmates who also had full-time jobs. The class was set up in clusters. I consistently got to work and study with a group of like-minded but differently experienced individuals. It was exciting to be in a continuous learning environment informed by the experiences of executives from Fortune 500 companies, doctors, lawyers, and entrepreneurs. Classroom time was only one full day per week, alternating Fridays and Saturdays for nineteen months. I had support from my manager and my team. They wanted this for me just as bad as I wanted it for me. There was even reimbursement support for tuition as part of our benefits program.

My MBA experience was transformational. There's the practical part of it, learning a new set of skills, concepts, and ideas that you can apply in real time at work. Then there's the social side of the program. Time around high-profile students in the classroom means that your whole intellectual horsepower starts to level up. It was a way to test my mettle. At Hampton, the academic part of my experience was important but was not always my top priority. Going back to school meant that I had a chance to readdress the idea that, when it came to learning at the postsecondary level, I could phone it in. This time, being the big man on campus wasn't my goal. This time, I had to do well for the sake of my family's security, my career, and the investment Pepsi had made in my future.

Our cluster jelled together even before classes started. I was lucky. The program began with an overnight retreat at an off-site location in the woods where we focused on getting to know each other and team building. Joe was my bunkmate. He was a seasoned sales executive, a little bit older, a little bolder than me. As soon as he found out we'd be working in teams, Joe scoped out the possibilities to create an inclusive and eclectic cluster. Richard was an engineer, not really outgoing but incredibly intelligent. Kathleen was IT-savvy and very buttoned-up, an entrepreneur and consultant. Chris was the youngest guy in the group next to me, also super sharp and highly energetic. Jon was a general manager at a family-owned company, being groomed to take over and run it one day. Robin was very strategic, and she provided great balance and objectivity for our group. I was the big company teammate who brought sales, marketing, and operations experience to the table. It felt like each of us had a specific contribution to make, one that would enhance our opportunities to both understand the materials and get decent grades on the projects and case studies we'd have to work on together.

Every Tuesday we'd have a study night at Jon's place in central Cincinnati, sometimes ending with a couple of beers, the one night a week I had a break from parenting duties. It was good timing for me in many ways. I didn't have to travel as much for my job then, because my market role was local. Together, we'd use those team huddles to work on group projects or prep each other for tests. I rarely missed a session.

Different vocabulary, different vibe, a whole lot more confidence. I learned that with an MBA, I was sharper. My network was growing. My image was changing.

All of a sudden I recognized that, back at work, I was getting attention that I hadn't been getting a year earlier because now I was blossoming and growing.

All of a sudden I was seeing a world of possibilities I had not had the chance to imagine before, and all of a sudden I was learning that the world was a beautiful place.

Xavier's program included trips abroad, half of the class going to Asia and the other to Europe, to work and present to partner universities and companies. My rising feeling of understanding my worth was why, when we went on that MBA trip, my golf clubs were with me. One of the most important reasons that I decided to get an MBA was that it opened my opportunities up internationally. But my instinct told me that I had to have balance. I had to create a space in which I would be able to be myself, lean in to a pace that made sense for me, open up possibilities rather than close them down in fear of not being seen as committed to my work. The perhaps not-too-surprising result was that combining golf with corporate presentations worked to my advantage in more ways than I had expected.

My classmates and I, those who had golfed together at St Andrew's, managed to get back to London on Sunday night. On Monday and Tuesday, we were in consultation meetings with Tesco, the UK's biggest supermarket chain, as well as some government agencies that regulated their business market, experiencing the full gamut of corporate negotiations. By Wednesday, we were on a plane to Munich to meet up with executives at BMW. Every night, we had business dinners and events, and by Friday, we were exhausted. Xavier had arranged for all of us to spend our final meetings in Germany on the following Monday, so that we could enjoy our last weekend in Europe before coming home to our families.

I wasn't going to waste a moment of it. I said to myself, "I'm going to go golf." I got on the subway. I had asked the concierge at the hotel where to go, and I was pointed in the direction of a club right within the city. I just picked up my golf bag and bought a subway ticket to the stop nearest the club, taking a taxi the rest of the way. People were staring at me. It was a novelty for Germans to see a tall Black man carrying golf clubs on a train, and I got a lot of double takes from people wondering if they'd just spotted Tiger in the wild. I ended up on the course with two older women in front of me. They offered me the chance to play through, but we ended up playing together and having a great time. After our round, they bought me drinks and later dropped me off at my hotel for my final business dinner. I could never get acclimated to the food in Germany—Munich seemed to be the sausage capital of the world—but it was one of the most exhilarating experiences of my life.

GOLF, TO ME, is more than just a game.

Since I started playing golf, I've spent thousands of hours on the course. My return on that time investment has been robust, both personally and professionally, and I'm a firm advocate of the sport for that reason. Golf can be a game changer in terms of relationships, access, and careers. And the earlier you start, the more opportunities you can have. Golf helps you to strengthen relationships, practice strategic planning, expand your network, find common ground with others, and nurture your well-being.

And golf is not just a white guy sport. It's an everyone sport.

Here are the facts. The National Golf Foundation reports that 25.6 million Americans played golf in 2022. Junior golfers (ages eight to eighteen) have grown to 3.4 million, up 36 percent since 2019. More than one-third of those juniors are young women, and 25 percent are non-white, compared to only 6 percent of junior players two decades ago. While I want those representation numbers to continue to grow, I'm seeing real progress on the green.

That's especially the case when it comes to women's golf.

Throughout my career, I've had the chance to play in hundreds of professional-amateur (pro-am) events all over the country, designed for executives to spend time with customers and play with some of the world's best golfers. Most of the events I played in were on the Ladies Professional Golf Association (LPGA) Tour at beautifully designed country club courses in Arizona, California, and Florida, spending time with some of the game's legends on and off the course. After I moved to Florida, my love for the women's game and the LPGA Tour grew even stronger. I developed a solid relationship with then-commissioner Mike Whan and with title-holder Annika Sörenstam and her husband, Mike McGee. I helped Pepsi lend its support to several high-profile events such as the CME Group Titleholders event and Solheim Cup. It's been remarkable to see the growth of the women's game globally, especially after we landed Annika a partnership deal with the Lipton Tea brand. From that deal, local grassroots efforts to introduce young women to the game were so much more successful.

I've been fortunate to play some of the best golf courses in the country, but without a doubt one of my most memorable experiences was in 2022 when I actually qualified to play in a full LPGA Tour event in Orlando during the Hilton championships. This was one of the more unique events on the circuit; we had high-profile celebrities join the tournament, which aired on national television. I played in the Wednesday pro-am event and shot a low enough score that I was one of several amateurs who qualified for the full field weekend competition with elite golfers and NFL, NBA, NHL, and tennis players, as well as other celebrities. I was not playing for actual prize money like the pros; I was competing against other amateurs.

It was a four-day event, so I cleared my calendar. I also needed a caddy, so I called my son Devon to assist. It was January in Florida, and although the mornings were cold and the playing field was intense, it was also a beautiful experience playing in the same with group elite tour players like Stacy Lewis and NFL Hall of Famer Charles Woodson.

Having won her first pro title in 2007, Stacy was just coming off a playoff victory in the Ladies Scottish Open in East Lothian, Scotland, in 2020, when we met. On the course, nothing phased her: the TV cameras, the noise, the fans asking for autographs. On the very first hole, I actually got a par, and after laughing about the fact that we shared the same last name, the champion allowed me to go ahead of her on the next tee because I had a better score. Golf is a sport grounded in etiquette connecting back to its nineteenth-century origins.

FOR ME, scrambling and joy are kindred spirits.

Having been drawn back into my shared history with Butch and Roland through their deaths, I spent a compressed period of time trying to control risks for my family, at work, and for myself. In Cincinnati, I went hard. Like my grandfather before me, and like many Black men and women, I pressed myself into overwork to ward off the ghosts of my family's past fears.

I am a big fan of sports. But in learning how to play a sport, and this *particular* sport, I altered the way that I approached the confrontations and demands of my life.

What I've learned about golf is that you can always get better. It's not possible to play a perfect game. You don't usually hit the mark of a hole in one, at least not often. What you can always do on a golf course is practice.

There is a serenity in arriving at a golf course, green and organized, in the midst of a big city or a small town. Golf puts each player in a situation where we have to start with a positive mindset. I can dial up my sense of accomplishment by crushing the game, but I can also dial down my fears.

Often at night, in my moments of quiet when I reflect on my day, I use golf as a way to process how I might change the way I would approach a challenge the next time I face it. There is peace in knowing that you can only hit one ball at a time, and that you have the space and time to make new, tiny choices each step of the way. There is a feeling of satisfaction in entering into a traditionally white territory, a members-only golf club, and knowing that you have the ability to turn heads not only by how you look but by how you play the game with confidence. In creating a golf practice, I found calmness in chaos.

I found myself.

16

HOT

THE COLA WARS were business on steroids.

After three years in Ohio, I had a decision to make. Do I go back to the beverage business where my roots are? Or do I continue on at Taco Bell, where I had traction and an opportunity to go to California and work in a corporate role? My instinct told me to stay with Pepsi. Yes, I still believed in the company. There were bigger things happening, though: the company was making moves that were revolutionizing not only the soft drink category but the entire consumer product field.

Why? Because out of any ultimate rival matchup you can think of, any battle of will and talent—Ali versus Frazier, Michigan versus Ohio State, Yankees versus Red Sox, Lakers versus Celtics—Pepsi versus Coke had them beat.

Since the drink that eventually became branded as Pepsi was invented in 1893 by pharmacist Caleb Bradham, only seven years after Coca-Cola was created, consumers have loved it. The Pepsi Challenge marketing push in the 1980s wasn't a gimmick; again and again it's been proven that people actually prefer the taste of Pepsi over Coke in blind taste tests. It's a case study that still shows up in business school courses today, and the results always seem to shock people. That's because people are in love with the idea of Coke, but they aren't necessarily in love with drinking it.

We certainly didn't need Coke, at least not in its original formula. John Pemberton, the inventor of Coca-Cola, was addicted to morphine, a natural opioid, and he used coca leaf as a so-called safer alternative. In the late nineteenth century when he was experimenting with beverage ideas, cocaine was widely endorsed as a cure-all for every ill. Pepsi was invented as a medical aid as well, but to treat dyspepsia, an upset stomach. Neither beverage did much for health, but they did taste good.

That's the conundrum of business as a whole: we buy things because of our emotional attachment to them, not because we necessarily need or even want them.

It's a fact that consumers' emotional needs are the reason that salespeople exist. In my years in business, I've learned that people associate a brand with an experience. It's absolutely true that colors, sound, and motion are connected with that experience in the form of advertising.

But even more important are the relationships we form that make the brand personal. People can easily turn down a product they don't like, but they won't deliberately disappoint a person they don't like. When the margins between Pepsi and Coke are so close, as they are in many markets around the United States, those relationships make all the difference.

Given that, the cola wars were the most extreme business challenge I have ever faced for one simple reason: it was a Super Bowl environment every day. If you look at the way that sports teams navigate their gameplay, all the work you put into your season is incremental as you prepare for that once-a-year big game or season-ending championship. With the cola wars, our sales teams carried that intensity every single moment we were at work. You're out to sell, gain space, increase market share, strengthen relationships; you're fighting for the same thing day in, day out. Consumers are going to make a choice: they'll either pick up your product or a competitive product, so you want to make sure it's your product.

Pepsi has a strong legacy, one that resonates with people who don't have a fondness for 1950s-era soda shops and saddle shoes, and for good reason.

But there is a middle ground. And the fact is that if Pepsi can win in one store on one street at a local level, you're building to win. That was a job I excelled at, and after MBA school and Taco Bell, I felt like I could make waves.

It helped that Pepsi's marketing team was riding those waves as well. In the mid-1990s, Pepsi had launched its most successful long-term strategy of the cola wars using the slogan "Drink Pepsi, Get Stuff." Our consumers could collect Pepsi Points on packages and cups that could be redeemed for free Pepsi merchandise. Pepsi Stuff was an instant success, and not surprisingly, it was easy to leverage on a store level until the whole concept blew up because someone acquired enough points to be awarded an AV-8B Harrier II jet. But in the '90s and '00s, Pepsi was also making effective moves in advertising with some of the most influential stars in the United States at the time, including Ray Charles, Cindy Crawford, Mariah Carey, Mike Myers, Beyoncé, and Britney Spears.

There was a momentum I wanted to be a part of, a momentum that led to the fastest narrowing of the gap between Pepsi and Coke in our long and competitive corporate histories.

And so, while I was wrapping up my MBA in 1998, I was transferred to Phoenix, Arizona, to come home to Pepsi.

PHOENIX IS hot as Hades, and in that job, it felt like the heat was always on.

There is a hidden part in a Pepsi job, and maybe any corporate job, in Phoenix. It's something most people wouldn't think about when it comes to career planning. Arizona is where a lot of C-suite executives have second homes, and I'm willing to bet that was even more the case in the '90s than it is today. Its mild winter climate is golfing and tennis heaven, and the state is more serene than Florida and closer to the action than Hawaii. Property taxes are substantially lower than the national average.

Reality is when you're working in Arizona, you're going to run into some bigwigs, and often. It's a good thing if you're up to the challenge, but if you're not, you're under the microscope. When I arrived, the business was not performing well. Phoenix and Denver were the two largest markets in our division. I was under even more pressure because the president of Pepsi North America had selected me for the job, mostly because he thought I might be the right person to turn things around given my experience in other challenger markets. The Great West Business Unit executives wanted a turnaround to happen immediately. They weren't wrong. I could see it too. In my first week there, I was going out into the market and I could see conditions were well below standard. The team was not running. They weren't even out in the stores. They were making excuses about everything.

My life had gotten complicated though. For the final eight weeks of my master's degree, I was taking red-eyes every Thursday or Friday night after work to come back to Sherene in Cincinnati and returning to Phoenix to start my work-week on Mondays. Sherene was pregnant with our second child, and I still had to attend classes on alternating Fridays or Saturdays while living in an entirely different state. Sherene couldn't even travel because of the late stage of her pregnancy, so she wasn't able to look at houses with me on the ground. I would take pictures and bring the film back to Ohio with me to develop them in a drugstore photo lab over the weekend, and she'd let me know what she liked and what wouldn't work. Back in Phoenix, I'd be out with a realtor after work, trying to get a home ready for her.

On the first Saturday in June, I was so exhausted I just wanted to sleep. I just got home from a red-eye flight from Phoenix, and as soon as Sherene opened the door to greet me, her water broke. I dropped my bag in the house and took her to the hospital. It was thirteen hours before she delivered our amazing daughter, Jordan, at eleven o'clock at night. We were just grinding, the two of us. We just kept going. I felt like it was just the two of us against the world because we had to pull each other up, be fully in that relationship, for every-thing to work.

And everything was not working, at least not at Pepsi.

The executive group, including the president, had shown up, and they had a different agenda. The president didn't want to see "setup" stores, the ones with a perfectly curated, Disney-like ambience that had been prepared ahead of time. Some teams would rationalize these kind of market tours, say-ing that they needed to demonstrate stores at their absolute best, but it was a charade and the president knew it. When my boss, Ron, put on his signal to turn right, the president asked him to turn left. Watching Ron's facial expression was price-less. I knew we would be in for quite the day. We ended up in random locations in some suburban trade areas, somewhere well outside the zone we had planned to show off.

"It was a disaster," I commiserated with Ron. "It was terrible. Terrible. After about three stores, maybe four stores, the president walked out. It was a walk of shame with each one of them. He's, like, let's go."

But the president wasn't wrong. It was the absolute right thing to do. We had to break the culture of setting up stores in advance of visits. Later, the president, Ron, and I were sitting in a Chevys, a little Tex-Mex restaurant. The president wanted to talk to us about how to get things back on track. It was a pep talk more than a butt-chewing, but we knew that he was very serious and there would be consequences if things didn't get fixed quickly.

"I know you're new in this market, Derek. Got a lot of confidence in who you are. We got to get this thing going. High expectations, but just get yourself organized. What do you think is going wrong, Derek?"

"I think it's all about the lack of fundamentals," I said. "We're not paying attention to the important details that make our business successful. From a selling, ordering, merchandising, and communications standpoint, we are just missing the mark at the store level. And the team has sort of accepted this as the norm. Just having routes covered seem to be where the bar is set each day, versus how well we're doing against our objectives and competition. Did we win or lose today? It's just that simple. Winners want to be surrounded by winners, plain and simple. If you are not carrying your weight, you are essentially a drag on team outcomes."

"You're right," the president said. "So what do you have to do?"

"Everything. We have to do absolutely everything."

"Yes, but we also have to prioritize. We've got to get this thing turned around, and you guys have got to work together and support each other. And I know you can do it, but we've got to start now. I'll be back in a couple of months. Right? You have some time. We'll check on your progress then."

I knew I had to lock and load. If Arizona needed fundamentals, I was going to give them fundamentals.

I had just come away from two major learning experiences: MBA school and Taco Bell. In both situations, what made all the difference was getting exposure to something bigger and better than myself. So, I had an idea that would produce the same effect for everyone under my management. I would create the look of success on such a grand scale that it couldn't be ignored, and it would also be a learning academy in which every sales team member would have to become certified in order to excel in the field.

The thirty-day Executional Excellence Academy built on everything I had created and explored in my Pepsi experience to date. What resources did we have? In Arizona, we had huge warehouse spaces, lots of merchandising equipment, and all the product we needed. I took over a section of one of our warehouses and, with my team, created a model store complete with coolers, gondolas, racks, vending machines, point-of-sale materials, etc.—all the things that we use and sell in real stores. I'd meet with the Large Format (Bulk) group, the Small Format group (Conventional), and the Vending group (On-Premise), our three sales force segments, every week, sitting them down in front of my wall projector with its acetate slides, reviewing merchandising standards. We covered brand flow, package placement, perimeter presence, proper rotation, correct POS usage—all of the fundamentals— walking through the model warehouse store.

"This is how every store will look, right?" I said to the team. "Every cooler, every piece of equipment, every store has to look like this. I need you to have absolute clarity and consistency on everything we do. The order you put Pepsi, Diet Pepsi, Mountain Dew, Slice on the shelves matters. Every move you make has to be deliberate and picture-perfect."

I meant picture-perfect *literally*. We had teams set up stores, take pictures, and compare them to what we had showed them back at the warehouse. When something was off-kilter, they had to change it, even old logos. I even had the team take tests on more challenging concepts like brand flow. Once the district managers were certified, they had sixty days to certify the market using the same training plan. I had evaluation forms for district managers to check off, looking at everything from marketing swag to the paper tags we used to place on each and every shelf of product.

"Everybody knows what the look of success is right now. I need to see this converted in stores. Right? Right," I said. "So let's give our best effort every day and watch what will happen. Get rid of the old and bring in the new, and after sixty days, we'll validate every store on every route."

What happened in the next sixty days was game-changing. We blew away our sales forecasts weekly. The key account manager team could not realize why they seemed to be under-forecasting each week. They knew what we were up to but had a hard time flowing it through the forecast.

That challenge we had balancing supply and demand swiftly moved in the opposite direction. All of a sudden, there was a strain on the production end of things, and the warehouse was not keeping up with what we needed in stores. We were consistently seeing more and more demand because the execution started coming together. The team had to learn how to round up efficiencies and start sending full pallets on every delivery.

I was elated at how it came together. We were getting our numbers, and we had the look of success. The executives that came back were shocked at what we had accomplished in less than two months. Even my boss was surprised at how things turned around.

"I got a call from one of the New York execs who was vacationing in Arizona about the store up in his neighborhood. He was there this month, and I didn't expect him out until the holidays," he confessed. "What did you do in that store?"

"Did he like what he saw?"

"Yes, I mean, he liked what he saw. Wow, Derek. You said we have the same route person, right? Well, how did this happen all of a sudden?"

I told him about the program.

"This thing's working?"

"Yes, sir," I said. "People were always looking for this direction. They just didn't know how to get there."

1999 was a great year. 2000 was an excellent year. Phoenix had become a contender, and everybody wanted to see what happened in that market. People from all over Pepsi were visiting to take note of the good vibe coming out of the city. People loved working there. The team was firing on all cylinders professionally and personally. We'd go to sporting events, play golf, or happy hours after work, building our culture and community. People felt good about coming into work. I was able to hire new management team members to expand the business because now we could afford to provide the kind of incentives that our team members wanted.

That's when the floodgates opened, and I realized that I had a real gift for getting things right, and that maybe that feeling that I was at the top of my game, always, wasn't a mistake. I had been thrown into underperforming situations time and again and had gained a reputation for creating a turnaround plan that worked every time: Baltimore; Washington, DC;

Cincinnati; and now Phoenix. I was getting opportunities for promotion based on the fact that I had worked out a system for performance not just for myself but for dozens, then hundreds, and eventually thousands of Pepsi employees.

BY THE TIME we had settled in Phoenix, Sherene and I had worked and lived in three cities in the seven years since we had gotten married.

Once we got into the groove of living in a new city, we had to start all over again. Three years after Phoenix we were in Portland, Oregon, and three years after that we moved to Denver, Colorado. On each move, we had to work at being accepted as someone's new neighbors. We were a younger Black couple moving into increasingly affluent neighborhoods, and pretty soon we noticed that we were being socially categorized as an athlete and his wife rather than as two up-and-coming executives moving up the corporate ladder. It wasn't easy to find a Black salon or barbershop in a majority-white community, but once we did, that became a place of comfort. We weren't close enough to our fraternity or sorority back home, but we did reach out to Black organizations like Jack and Jill, Alpha Kappa Alpha, and Kappa Alpha Psi to find a sense of connection. We got to be ourselves, be part of the culture, hear the music we liked, and speak the language we were comfortable using. We carved out room for ourselves as much as we could. And in every city, we got invited to parties and drinks with our neighbors on the block.

But we were never really on the inside. We never really dove deep into the culture of the neighborhoods we lived in, because we weren't there long enough.

Moving from city to city, we weren't lonely, but we were on our own journey together. Sherene and I continued to be distanced from our parents, families, fraternity friends, and childhood friends. It wasn't deliberate, but we had a plan in motion. We had each other, we had our children, and we had work. My education was finished, and I didn't have my Tuesday night study sessions anymore. Email was for work, and there was no Facebook or Instagram yet. Sherene and I were no longer caught up in the day-to-day drama of other people's lives.

But while I kept in touch with my mother and brother and some of the Kappas, we were no longer as close as we once were. I realized that we had lost some of those who had been associated with the most pain, like Butch and Roland, who had held so much of my attention and fears. In getting away from my family ties, I realized how psychologically binding they had been, not because I did not love my mom and brothers, or even my father, but because they had been living in a frozen state of mind, one that I had unconsciously emulated. My mother had worked in the same place for decades because it was the safe choice, the only choice, the location where she had hours to be on her own, where she did not have to worry about someone coming in the door with a gun or a bag of heroin, where her responsibilities were set out for her, where the rules never changed. That safety was deserved, is something that she and everyone needs, but she didn't create it for herself; she stayed tied to that spot in her anxiety, without hoping for anything more. It was a blessing for Damon and for me because we benefited from the security her job created, but it was a curse, a purgatory at the very least, for Mom's true desires, whatever those ought to have been. She never let herself find what she wanted. She only let herself survive.

Getting away, for me, meant that I was able to move beyond that, beyond mere survival. I knew I needed to pivot and, in doing so, advance. Our new family was humming and running on all cylinders in part precisely because of that distance, precisely because of my ability to step away from the past. My past, my family story, was complicated and painful, and it didn't serve us, didn't serve me.

The present was simple.

Inside Pepsi, a lot of my days just looked like blue versus red. That simplicity masked the true effort and creativity it took to focus absolutely and utterly on disrupting Coke's flow: its market share, its influence, and its profit potential. With the luxury of working in so many different places, I got to see a little bit of everything. I got to know the consumer better and what drove purchase intent and loyalty. I got to build world-class relationships with customers to grow our collective businesses. I got to work in the trenches with our associates to help make, move, sell, and market our portfolio. I got to support the communities that I worked in to lift others up. I learned how to fight harder in places like Phoenix. As more competitors arose, of course the battle was no longer just about colas. As the millennium turned, we had to deal with other key competitors like Red Bull, Snapple, Nestea, and the rising tide of beverages made with high-fructose corn syrup.

It was fascinating to develop business strategies in all those cases, because they're all different. You can't run the same play in every game. I learned that I had to be very precise in my strategies, but that I also needed to build a team of assertive, confident people who knew how to overcome their own fears.

In Arizona, I had created a pathway for people to feel good about who they were and where they were going. The Executional Excellence Academy set up a blueprint for our team members to follow a path set out for them, to build working relationships in a way where they didn't just feel supported, they knew they were supported. I was deliberate about relationship management, both inside and outside of the company.

There was continuity on the job. There were clear expectations. Everyone knew where they stood, and what they could do to follow that same pathway that I had laid out for them.

I had to lay out a new pathway for myself as well.

For much of my career, I had one game plan in mind: flawless execution of the tasks set out before me. By 2000, my results and my reputation for success meant that my name was being considered for some general manager jobs, the kind where my geographic reach would be much bigger and my ideas could scale up in a cluster of towns and cities. I'm not talking about managing millions of consumer product sales but hundreds of millions. But making it to general manager had been the absolute summit of my career goals at Pepsi. Back at Hampton when I had given up the idea of being a spy to accept a role at the company, a general manager position had seemed like an impossible dream. There were a lot of Black sales managers, but very few people had continued up the ladder to the rung where I was clearly headed.

I had to see myself as the leader I was becoming, rather than the guy who did everything right so that he wouldn't miss a beat.

I had to establish a vision of my own potential, which very few individuals like me had explored before.

It was time to advance.

17

FUTURE PROOF

WHEN I WAS in high school in DC, let's just say I lived for clothes.

I washed everyone's clothes. That was one of my primary household jobs when my mom was at work. Everything had to come out of the washing machine and onto the clotheslines in the basement and the yard, because the dryer never worked. Hanging socks, hanging underwear, hanging shirts, hanging jeans. It was damp down in the basement but it was warm, so no matter what, the clothes eventually dried out, and I'd fold them and put them away. Everything back then was cotton, or maybe cotton and polyester. I tried my best not to have to do the ironing as well, but I couldn't show up at school without my uniform on, which included pressed trousers, a button-up shirt, and a tie.

On the weekends, especially once I started thinking about girls, I knew I had to get some better clothes for myself. It was the '80s, and everyone was wearing polo shirts. And when I say polo shirts, back then we only meant Ralph Lauren with the little polo player insignia. I didn't know those short-sleeve, piqué knit, front-placket shirts were actually invented by René Lacoste for tennis in the 1930s, but Izod Lacoste alligator–trademark shirts were even further out of my financial league than Ralph's hundred-dollar, brightly colored designs. Lacoste had made the collar soft so it could be easily flipped up as needed to protect the back of his neck from direct sunlight; popping the collar was part of the original design.

My friends and I found imitation Ralph Lauren polos for less than ten dollars, and they looked exactly the same as the original. They had the same stitches, the same name on the tag, and that was all that mattered. We had to catch the subway and then a bus to this place in Silver Spring, Maryland, with all of its Asian shops on Georgia Avenue, to get ourselves shirts in as many colors as we could afford.

We were buying the value version of the brand that we wanted to represent. Polos were Ivy League style, but at the time, the preppy look was not only popular among college attendees; it was also co-opted by the punk, skate, and especially the rap and hip-hop scenes. Ralph represented the Hamptons and wealth. We may have never been to ski lodges, but DC kids were grabbing it and repping it. Wearing a polo from a discount shop was how we could stay relevant. We couldn't keep up with the people who could afford the real thing, but we had found our look.

In Chocolate City, there were a fair number of households with two parents, but like me, most of my friends had just a single parent, which was usually the mom. Saving money where we could was just how it was. Some days I felt like I had it better than my friends; some days I didn't. I didn't feel in any sense that I was luckier than somebody else, but we weren't destitute. I didn't have a lot of resources, but I could hustle and make a buck here and there and be okay. We lived in a small row house, and I had my own bedroom and a black-and-white TV.

But throughout my childhood, my father being who he was, I did feel a loss. I felt that I didn't have the advantage of being a real kid, a kid who had a bedtime and a schedule and a dinner table where his dad would drop wisdom on him while they ate a real family meal. And I felt lonely because there were kids who had a better situation than me, whose parents could sign them up for team sports and drive them to the rec programs and afford the fees for uniforms. I saw those kids jump in their carpools, waving goodbye, while I had to turn around and walk home because I had two young brothers I had to watch all afternoon, all evening long, while I did the laundry.

As a child, I felt like I had all this potential and I couldn't leverage it.

It wasn't about the polo shirts I couldn't afford. That longing, that loss I was feeling, was about not knowing how to be the man I wanted to become. When I was young, I didn't have an adult I could look up to the way those carpool kids did. I was getting things done because I was figuring things out for myself and making up my own processes, testing to make sure they worked, but losing out on that pat on the back, that helping hand.

People like Earl Graves and Kevin Heath had stepped up to the plate, and their friendships literally changed the way that I dressed, that I held myself to honor, that allowed me to create a future I actually wanted. When I went to MBA school, the mystique of my colleagues who had earned their degrees at predominantly white institutions and/or Ivy League schools seemed to evaporate as well, and I didn't feel at odds with everyone else at the table. When I shifted the status quo in Phoenix and turned an underperforming market into a template for winning, my method of figuring things out for myself and making up my own processes was no longer reflective of a personal loss; it was a massive professional asset. I had all this potential and I knew now that I could leverage it. There could be no more separation between the Silver Spring polos and the Ralph Laurens.

I was going to be future proof.

WE MOVED between Phoenix, Portland, and then Denver in just over eight years. During that period of my life, I put together new teams, managed emerging Pepsi objectives, and—when I became the Vice President of Retail Sales for the Great West Business Unit at the Pepsi Bottling Group (PBG) in Colorado—helped deliver over $2 billion in net revenue to the company every fiscal year. It was one turnaround situation after another. Every new job and city required me to increase my leadership capacity at work, but even though I had risen to the VP level and was working in a broader region each step of the way, I was still expanding on the fundamentals: results, relationships, reputation. I had a really strong methodology in place, something that I could count on. Something that worked.

When I was promoted to VP, Consumer and Category Insights, in 2006, I didn't especially want to move to Somers, New York, to work at Pepsi headquarters. Being at HQ means being under the microscope. It's an expensive place to live. There is little flexibility or freedom. You're up there with just some super-sharp minds, not feeling yourself. And just as we were getting settled in Denver, we were getting ready for the arrival of our youngest child. Once again, Sherene had to hold the fort back while I had to get a house for us for our move from Colorado to Connecticut.

My biggest worry before I left was I was great at my job in sales leadership, but suddenly and for the first time I was working outside of a geographical sales and production funnel. It was going to be strange not looking at the daily sales report any longer.

Headquarters was mainly a think tank, setting strategic direction for the company both short and long term. The near term still mattered, and if performance was off in any way, HQ would intervene to build solutions to improve outcomes.

The place ran like a well-oiled machine, embodying true functional excellence throughout. My role was to ensure our businesses' largest trade. We had an enterprise mindset, working on new product launches, merging roles and missions and new ideas for building the business. I had to build a stronger level of connectivity with our parent company's marketing department and develop new kinds of relationships with Pepsi's marketing organizations, as well as build more comprehensive insight into the role of research and development at the company.

The lens on the business was suddenly at a very wide angle, and it was my job to see everything from a distance so that I could take it all in.

My role, officially, reported into Pepsi Bottling Group North America President Rob King. At the time, PepsiCo owned a portion of PBG, which was traded on the New York Stock Exchange. We were the largest bottler for the Pepsi system. What we did had significant influence over the rest of the franchise system throughout the country.

PepsiCo was essentially BrandCo. It provided the concentrated marketing muscle. PBG was OpCo. It produced, sold, and executed the portfolio. Being aligned and joined at the hip meant everything in terms of how much success we would have as a part of an integrated global Pepsi team.

It was my job as the head marketer for the system's largest bottler to ensure PBG, PepsiCo, and the franchise system were all on the same page in terms of our collective brand building, innovation, and execution platforms and performance expectations. The only way we would be successful was if we ensured there were never any win-lose scenarios across the key stakeholder groups. For marketing and most other functions, we leveraged joint committee structures; people were empowered to make decisions for their sector. This kept things in the pipeline moving and allowed us to set the right course of action on the business for both short- and long-term cycles.

This role was a huge undertaking for me. I always used to say I went from telling time backward and forward in field roles to building a clock inside out at HQ. I was in charge of making that happen everywhere, every day.

I remember my very first day going into the office. People from every functional team were dropping off binders full of corporate assets: supply chain, finance, sales, strategy, and more.

"Welcome to New York. Here you go," they'd say.

"Okay, thanks," I said, putting each binder to one side. "Nice to meet you."

My executive assistant poked her head around the door.

"Hey, just got a call from the boss's office. You're going with the boss, chief customer officer, and the chief strategy officer to St. Louis in three days."

"Three days."

"Yes."

"I gotta go through all these binders then."

"You gotta go through all these binders. Before wheels up," she added, nodding.

There was a lot to absorb. My top priority was to ensure our current brands and innovation pipeline were being built to effectively drive profitable topline growth and market share gains. Sports and music were huge levers for our business on both a national and local level. We understood that we could connect with consumers through both platforms, through the media, through merch, through events, and through day-to-day market collaborations.

From a time-management standpoint, we were in the middle of our financial cycle, and I had to jump in quickly and get integrated into those processes with my team. I had inherited a team that had been there for a while, but my most senior marketer had been running the department on an interim basis.

Right away, I could tell he was very disappointed that he didn't get the job. To him and a few others, I wasn't a natural marketer. I didn't come from their neck of the woods. Heck, I was almost ten years removed from my last marketing class. While I was no classical marketer, I knew our business cold and had posted strong results throughout my career. That was why I was brought to HQ. My capacity to learn and lead was strong. I didn't initially realize it, but this was the best job possible for me.

At the same time, like every other job before this one, I was tasked with cleaning this situation up. My role was to rebuild the whole thing so that we'd be more successful out in the field. I had worked on the ground across most of the United States, and I knew that the same old tools weren't working.

Going through the binders, I could see just how much I didn't yet know about this end of the business. I was rushed. I was under the gun, and I wanted to get it right. Despite being the new guy in town, I had to rely on my team to bring me up to speed, and within the first month of my tenure, we had to begin preparing for a big annual operating plan meeting with PepsiCo.

Eric Foss, our CEO, put a check-in meeting on the calendar to see our initial draft and overall perspectives. I asked my team where we were with our work. They handed me a deck they had been working on, and I used that to represent the department at the first check-in.

It didn't quite work out the way I had hoped.

Each of the C-suite executives was going through all of our various functional plans. When it was my turn for marketing, I started going through the first couple of pages and I could see the looks on the faces of the top brass.

Eric looked at the strategy officer and said, "Haven't we seen this before?"

"My team pulled this together. They had been working on this deck for a couple weeks, and this is our current thinking."

I didn't know it, but I had taken the bait.

"This is not going to work for us, Derek. Go back and take another cut that reflects new thinking and direction," he said. "This looks like last year's version with a new cover page."

It was my own fault. I knew there hadn't been time to create a new deck in a matter of days, but I took the easiest path forward. On one level, I should have absolutely been able to rely on a group of people who had been in this game for years and had collective expertise in this field and an obligation to their company to do their best work. On another level, I hadn't thought the whole thing through. I was an outsider, someone who was different in more ways than one. I trusted that the team would always put me in a good situation. It wasn't that they wanted me to fail, but the reality was they were stuck in an old model. Our company was moving in a different, faster direction that required leveled-up thinking, not the status quo, old-school network comfort that this group historically survived on.

"My apologies, I own this and will turn this around quickly," I said. I couldn't say anything else.

"Look, we all brought you here," Eric said, compassionately. "We brought you here for your experience, your ideas, your drive. We didn't bring you here to use the same old playbook. We want to see everything you've learned in the field. We want you to bring that approach and thinking experience to this job here. You understand how our business operates, and we want you to put the best effort forward to drive a renewed strategic approach. You, Derek Lewis, are here for a reason."

I needed to hear that call to action.

I walked out with a new mission. I had been let down, but I should have known better. This fell on me. I was going to play the game my way now. From that point forward, I was going to own it.

Right away I started taking charge, digging deeper into consumer insights, understanding how to approach the future for our big brands and categories. With the help of key stakeholders at PepsiCo, the franchise community, our field organization, and HQ mentors, I was able to develop a much clearer sense of the strategic direction we needed, and I recognized that we needed to get the right structure, the right capabilities, and the right tactical plans in place to make sure we could execute the strategy. I couldn't have what happened in my first meeting happen again. As much as I blamed myself, we needed a culture of new thinking, collaboration, and diversity. Out with the old and in with the new. To do that, we had to make some significant talent changes. Change in culture starts with leadership walking the talk.

I called up my human resources partner, Brian.

"I would like to reconstruct the HQ marketing organization to allow us to be best in class on brand building, innovation, and execution throughout the enterprise. We make ourselves better; we make everyone else better. To do that, I'm going to completely restructure the team, including titles and roles. And we're going to be a much more diverse team."

"Let's go do it," he replied. "Let's make this exciting."

Together, Brian and I created a communication package and started pitching our new plan to every business unit in the country, flying out to meet every business unit general manager, VP of sales, and head of marketing. We received 100 percent buy-in from every meeting. People knew we needed to change in order to level up. When we got back to HQ after every meeting, I had a slew of new inputs that helped me shape and refine my core message. Each time I made a presentation in the field, my communication strategy got better and better. It helped that I spoke their language. Out in our business units, these were my people, and I could trust their insight into what I had to say.

I was ready to come back to headquarters. I had taken to the road for two months, and I was ready.

"Okay, where are you at, Derek?" The C-suite was ready to hear what I had to say.

"I have a foolproof and future-proof plan. It includes a new marketing mission and vision, new structure, new operating principles, and new talent."

"Wow. Okay. Take us through it."

I walked them through my presentation. As I was looking around the room at the key players, I could see heads nodding. That is always a good sign.

"Have you shopped this around with the teams?" I was asked.

"I've walked them through it, and I have everyone on board. We've run everything through legal, HR. Everybody has checked out the whole plan. We've collected feedback in every business unit in North America. Every level in the organization is ready to go."

It wasn't an approach the company was used to. I had everything lined up ahead of time.

"It's aggressive," our president said. "Are we going too fast? This is a big move."

I could see their minds ticking away. They had to reconcile with this.

"Now I'm looking for your endorsement to go forward with it," I said, breaking the silence.

"Yeah, we want to go forward," he said, looking directly at me. "We'll move this forward."

The room was electric. People were calling out ideas.

"What's your thought position on timing?"

"Want a mentor to help out?"

"Call me if you need me!"

I could see heads nodding and people taking notes. When we rolled out the changes and the new organization, I hosted everyone in Las Vegas at our new team kickoff event. We invited media agencies, business partners, bottlers, everyone to be part of the experience. They were all part of our team. It was a world-class event and rollout that led to tremendous success for the function and company as a whole in the following year. I began to feel, act, and think like a marketer now. As a result, I began to join our executive team on investor roadshows to present to and meet with industry stakeholders. A year earlier, the thought of doing this had been absolutely nerve-racking to me. Now I felt as if I belonged and could move the needle. On occasion, I even got to represent our businesses in Mexico, Turkey, and Spain when my peers were unavailable to travel. Great things started to happen all around me.

This was powerful. This was power.

Spending some time with NBA mega-superstar LeBron James at a Nike EYBL Peach Jam event in North Augusta, SC, in 2021

TOP: Kicking it with the legendary ESPN College GameDay crew in Phoenix, AZ, for the Miami vs. Ohio State National Championship game in 2003
BOTTOM: Throwing up the "U" with Michael Irvin, Pro Football Hall of Famer, at a business event in Dallas, TX, in 2016

TOP: Meeting with Coach Nick Saban (second from right) during an official recruiting visit for my daughter at the University of Alabama in 2015

LEFT: Touring the New England Patriots' locker room while visiting with team executives and colleagues in 2017

RIGHT: Getting some pregame insights from sports commentator Maria Taylor at a Louisville vs. Notre Dame game in Louisville, KY, in 2019

TOP: Jordan and me at the Men's Final Four in Houston, TX, in 2023, the tenth time we attended the event together

BOTTOM: Celebrating Grant Hill's Naismith Basketball Hall of Fame enshrinement in Springfield, MA, in 2018 with Grant (second from right) and his wife, singer-songwriter Tamia

TOP: Awarding the MTN Dew 3-Point Contest trophy to Buddy Hield during the 2020 NBA All-Star weekend in Chicago, IL

BOTTOM: Awarding the MTN Dew 3-Point Contest trophy to Allie Quigley during the 2022 WNBA All-Star weekend in Chicago, IL. L to R: WNBA Commissioner Cathy Engelbert, me, Allie Quigley, and ESPN's Holly Rowe

FACING TOP: Hanging at an Orlando Magic game with Team Hayes (left) and Shaquille O'Neal

FACING MIDDLE: Laughing it up with Charles Barkley at NBA All-Star weekend in 2017

FACING BOTTOM LEFT: Chopping it up with Jayson Tatum at NBA All-Star weekend in 2022

FACING BOTTOM RIGHT: Welcoming Zion Williamson to Team MTN Dew

TOP LEFT: Hanging with A'ja Wilson at NBA Summer League in 2018

TOP RIGHT: Jordan and me celebrating Brittney Griner's jersey retirement in 2024

BOTTOM LEFT: Capturing a moment with 2021 WNBA All-Star MVP Arike Ogunbowale in Las Vegas, NV

BOTTOM RIGHT: Sherene and me hanging with Nancy Lieberman at BIG3 Finals in 2022

TOP: Orlando Magic CEO Alex Martins presenting me with my Pepsi retirement jersey in 2023

BOTTOM: Kellan presenting his hand-painted artwork to Orlando Magic star and 2022 NBA Rookie of the Year Paolo Banchero (second from left)

TOP LEFT: Sherene and me with Remy Ma in Miami, FL, during Super Bowl weekend 2020

TOP RIGHT: Hanging with Snoop Dogg after he hosted and DJed the Rookie of the Year Party at Super Bowl weekend 2020

BOTTOM: Me presenting the 2019 Pepsi NFL Rookie of the Year award (Nick Bosa winner) to Joey Bosa (center) with former Pepsi ROY Saquon Barkley onstage in Miami, FL

TOP LEFT: Me visiting one of Atlanta's most popular restaurants, Slutty Vegan, with founder and CEO Pinky Cole Hayes

TOP RIGHT: Me visiting with Virginia "Mama Ali," owner and cofounder of one of Washington DC's most famous and historic restaurants, Ben's Chili Bowl

BOTTOM: Hanging with Derrick Hayes, founder and CEO of rapidly growing Big Dave's Cheesesteaks, a business that I franchised beginning in 2024

TOP: Chilling with global soccer legends Ricardo Kaká (left) and Radamel Falcao in Orlando, FL, the night before a big match

LEFT: Going behind the scenes at Daytona International Speedway before the big race in 2023

RIGHT: Introducing Jeff Gordon, one of the best and most influential drivers in NASCAR history, before an event at Pepsi HQ in Somers, NY

Me fly-fishing in Aspen, CO, enjoying a unique blend of natural beauty and tranquility

TOP LEFT: Kicking it with then-Jackson State University QB Shedeur Sanders before a conference game in Jackson, MS, in 2021

TOP RIGHT: Wishing Coach Prime (Deion Sanders) good luck before a big home conference game in Jackson, MS, in 2022

BOTTOM: Coach Prime and me discussing the upcoming season during Southwestern Athletic Conference Football Media Day in 2022

Me completing my first and only Tough Mudder race in Florida in 2013. What an accomplishment!

Me getting cancer-free results after my colorectal surgery

Honored to have received a proclamation from Orange County Mayor Jerry Demings' office declaring 2/25/2023 Derek Lewis Day for decades of leadership and devoted service to the community

18

HIGHER UP

NEW YORK was like getting a PhD in Pepsi. I knew I had a lot of work to do, but I was very confident that I had the tools to do my job properly. It was a high-profile, high-bar environment. The trick was to adapt to that environment and become a high-bar player myself. I felt like I was a very senior leader in a big company. And I felt like I had the juice. Getting things done around HQ wasn't easy. You had to be built for this.

Even better, people wanted to spend time with me. They'd call me in for input, to get my point of view. I was seen as a player. They wanted my expertise. They wanted my strategy. They wanted my creativity. Some just wanted my energy. I had nothing to do with the branding, the look and feel of Pepsi, but I was not surprised when, two years after I started in New York, the company was launching its first new logo overhaul in twenty years. We were on fire.

That's when I knew I had the chance to move the needle.

What was the future of human resources at Pepsi?

I had been actively connected to many people at Hampton for social purposes, which had changed when we moved out west. So far away from our roots, Sherene and I started to see the potential in how we interacted with Black professional network organizations when and if we could. But now, back east and closer to home, I started to think about what I could do not only to help our family feel secure but to bridge gaps for other Black people, for all people of color, and for women who had the drive but not the luck or advantage of access due to background or education.

I wanted to lift up graduates who, like me, had to overcome so many social, economic, and personal barriers just to get through college.

The fact that our son Kellan was born just as we were arriving in New York in 2006 was also part of the equation, the push, the feeling of knowing that we had a lot at stake in the future of Black excellence. With Devon's, Jordan's, and now Kellan's futures in front of us, Sherene and I knew that Team Lewis had to reach beyond what we could do inside the walls of our home. We had gotten somewhere. We had clout, influence, and we were starting to reach a broader community. If we did not lift others up, we would have failed in our commitment to ourselves and our children. And we were hearing rumblings about this young Black senator in Chicago making an impact in politics.

Maybe it was time. Just maybe.

If we made it happen, if we could find a way to bring everyone into the fold, could we change our world?

ALL OF MY LIFE, I've been big on history. More than anything, I know my own Black history and I know Pepsi's history.

The way that someone becomes successful as an employee or even as an entrepreneur starts very early in their life.

History tells us that richer school districts and even states, where homes are more valuable, have more revenue derived from taxation to contribute to their schools to add extra-curricular programs and more experienced teachers. The flip side is that less desirable schools are characterized as having limited parental involvement and high teacher attrition, and they're generally perceived as being worse off socially and economically.

In a place like DC in the 1970s, these limitations absolutely would have affected most of the Black kids in my neighbor-hood. Most kids would have been living at arm's length from white society over the course of their educational lives.

The problem is, as researchers tell us, that educational social contexts at the elementary and secondary level lead to challenges all along the spectrum of education at the postsec-ondary level. Black students have shared a common historical experience characterized by limited educational resources to meet the needs and demands of the Black population for higher education. While HBCUs were able to fulfill that role, something changed over the course of history. The Great Depression and World War II left many Black colleges in financial crisis. Despite earlier improvements in funding, most land-grant HBCUs were still grossly underfunded when com-pared to their primarily white counterparts. While *Brown v. Board of Education* and the Higher Education Act of 1965, which ended segregation in schools, provided HBCUs with better funding to keep the doors of educational opportunity open, the fact that they are only identified according to a fed-eral definition necessarily limits the total number of colleges and universities eligible to receive federal funds.

All of this means that HBCUs have to rely on their alumni to build up money to expand their services. But given the barriers Black kids face getting ready for college in the first place, going all the way back to elementary school, it's pretty obvious how difficult building this kind of funding is likely to be. State funds are lower too: states provided roughly 40 percent less for HBCUs than for predominantly white colleges. Even after the Pell Grants were introduced to level the financial playing field for Black students to pay for their education, things didn't change that much.

Out of all HBCUs in the United States, only three—Howard University, Spelman College, and my own Hampton University— have been able to acquire endowments in the top three hundred of all US institutions of higher education.

This hidden challenge started to arise in my consciousness the more time I spent hiring people, helping revamp Pepsi's on-campus recruitment strategies, and trying to build truly diverse and comprehensive teams.

But here's the thing: HBCUs are more successful at meeting the academic and social needs of Black students. HBCU students have a more positive self-identity than their counterparts at other schools. They are more likely to graduate from college, especially Black men, who are the most vulnerable to leaving school before they finish. HBCU students are more likely to go on to get a master's degree or a PhD.

Why? Research shows that students at HBCUs benefit more from the social support networks on their campuses than they do from similar groups at predominantly white colleges. They feel good about going to school. They feel psychologically and culturally supported. Their life choices are affirmed rather than corrected.

Historically, HBCUs are better for Black students.

I knew this intuitively. My own experience of feeling accepted and emotionally supported at Hampton made it clear to me that there was massive value in being a part of an HBCU. There was nothing in the world like the ease in being able to speak my own culture and language and beliefs. As Sherene and I moved through seven different states with varying levels of access to other Black families and professionals, we were missing that camaraderie. We were able to code-switch easily into a broader and more diverse community, and we valued being able to do that, but the comfort of being among people who knew what we knew, were who we were, wasn't there.

Like my own family growing up, there is a lot left unsaid when it comes to the intersection of Black history and our personal histories. The little stresses that work their way into the food that we buy and make; the extra time we spend on buses and walking, instead of driving, to make ends meet; the aggressions, micro and obvious, we constantly face that bring us down and make us feel small, even for a moment. They add up. They add up in real time. And it takes generations upon generations for us to find the right coping mechanisms to get through, to get by, to get up. So even someone born today will still be carrying those family experiences when they turn outward into the American workplace. At the same time, Black graduates have to be proud of our history, our starting point, and how we have carried ourselves to that next level. HBCUs make all the difference in recognizing that, in generating graduates who understand their role in the continuum of Black excellence.

It isn't just about me. When I started to understand why HBCUs mattered so much on an institutional level, something else clicked. I began to recognize that there was much more I had to do to balance the playing field at Pepsi.

When I got settled in in New York, and in the years to come, I would purposely set up visits to bring senior Pepsi managers on campus to get them experienced in understanding the lives of Black students. Listening to their language. Appreciating their cultural norms. I'd have them walk around a campus where you see nothing but Black kids going to class or going into the student union.

"I want you to see this world because it does exist," I said to my colleagues. "We need to be here more often and need to recruit here. We need to lean in more here."

I used my social capital to create a belief, and a culture, of total acceptance of diversity and its value to the company because when you deal with hiring diverse candidates, you hear a lot of very cliché things about fitting potential employees into established boxes.

"It's not minorities per se, but if they don't have the experience, why invest in them?"

"They didn't go to an Ivy League school like this other candidate."

"They lack strategic horsepower."

The more boxes that could be ticked, the more likely a candidate would be considered for the job. How are people supposed to get ahead if you always make them fit into a set of criteria established by people in positions of power, trickled down over multiple generations into the profile standards that we expect today? My response was to create more boxes. Does someone's alma mater define how strategic they are, or can you ask them how they would answer a strategic question in an interview? Are we going to make a good candidate wait to get promoted, or can we put them in a strategic role that stretches them and mentor them into leveling up?

There is nothing wrong with being transparent with employees, whether Black or Hispanic or white, about what you need from them. If I could see the potential in someone, I'd set them up for success so that the choice to advance was theirs, not mine.

"So you're gonna go into this role," I would say to my new hires. "Here is what we're looking for from you. Here are the skills and the activities you need to get on top of in order to demonstrate a high level of performance. You are going to be very heavily graded in this role. Do you understand what you're signing up for? Do you know what you're up against? If you're feeling challenged at any time, come to me for advice. I'm here to support you."

THERE IS a continuum that I'm a part of, that my wife belongs to, and that shapes my children's lives, and that is the legacy of not only slavery, but the laws and the social values that were created alongside it. That legacy contributed to the code of survival that my father created for my brothers and me, and it molded the ways in which my mother and her parents kept their heads down, kept small and quiet in their government jobs in order to feel safe, to sit as far below notice as they could, to get by and get on with it.

Getting an education and moving toward visible success was my own act of resistance not *against* my family, but *for* my family, past and future. I had long ago decided that I would not stay small or hidden. I would be who I wanted to be, on my own terms. I would advance. I would be able to offer my family the protection of a corporate salary, a sense of pride, a piece of the community pie, a course-corrected legacy.

But Black history shows us that there is a lot that we have not taken into consideration when it comes to understanding who is allowed to advance, factors that go far beyond legislation and efforts at equity in the social sphere.

Business leaders who are serious about equity need to understand where their applicants come from: their personal, professional, and educational histories. By this I don't mean that every potential employee has to hand over a memoir. Equity is not something that can be achieved inside a company after someone is hired. It starts when an individual is provided with the kind of equal life opportunity that will allow them to not only thrive but to give back to their community so that the cycle continues.

Think about it. If Pepsi was to continue to recruit from Hampton, which it did and does, then it is not only creating a pathway into Pepsi for new employees. By recruiting there, Pepsi is also creating the potential for Hampton to continue to reap the benefits of its alumni contributions to the school. This, in turn, provides Hampton with increased power to support Black students and their future success.

And it goes both ways. Companies that recruit at HBCUs not only get access to candidates, they are also able to connect with students who have a greater than average chance of feeling socially, psychologically, and culturally affirmed, who have confidence in their own skins. Who can see themselves free to contribute to Pepsi's success, to be in a high-profile, high-bar environment and not doubt themselves, not succumb to imposter syndrome. Who can level up.

The same is true for all corporations that look at Black culture with interest, and most do, because the combined spending of Black households has increased 5 percent annually over the past two decades, according to 2021 data from consulting firm McKinsey. Companies are leaving money on the table when it comes to Black consumers, according to 2022 data. Black consumers' collective economic power is set to expand dramatically, from about $910 billion in consumption in 2019 to $1.7 trillion in 2030. Right now, however, $300 billion of that value has yet to be captured by American companies in serving Black interests. A lot of the gaps have to do with basic unfulfilled wants: Black consumers want higher access to the food and beverages they like, the entertainment experiences they desire, and the housing options that suit their lifestyles.

This is why Pepsi, in identifying and connecting with Black employees and consumers at the same time, is able to fill that gap. Pepsi has always embraced the Black community. They've done it from day one, better than anybody else, longer than anybody else. Pepsi doesn't take credit enough for how long their commitment to Black America has been truly evident in their hiring practices and in their excitement about Black culture and its promise.

At the same time, what I found when I moved back to the East Coast and started trying to increase awareness about the value of partnering with HBCUs was that some of Pepsi's momentum in the Black community had been lost. The reason? A lot of talk about emerging demographic trends in the Hispanic community in the United States, something that's important but not more important than the Black market or any other demographic target market. When you look at the numbers using the same McKinsey methods, both markets represent a total of around a billion dollars in consumer demand.

What's the problem, then?

Diversity can't be about fads. Businesses need a better pipeline to people, to stakeholders. This includes people who buy these products and people who will sell these products. Former Pepsi-Cola CEO Walter S. Mack was a trailblazer for the Black community when he hired the first all-Black sales team in 1940. Mack proved that building teams that truly represent consumers can lead to more equal product experiences and more representation across the board. Over my career, I learned that being wired into the community can help you on many levels. You attract people to your business, learn about business opportunities, and develop a presence in the community. It's a win-win situation.

At home and at the office, there needs to be real, authentic conversations about the root causes of why many businesses struggle so much with diversity and equity. There has to be a holistic recognition that racial inequality has long existed in our country, and while much progress has been made, there is still much work left to be done. Real change can only occur when all of us recognize and commit to taking the tangible steps to effect that change. It's not simply about hiring more people of color. It's about accepting a willingness to lead and an openness to bring others along the journey.

Diversity is the one thing we all have in common. If we can get everyone to recognize that we each bring something unique to the table, there will be an unparalleled level of unity and teamwork. Each of us is unique—that's what we have in common. If everyone could acknowledge and appreciate our differences, we will be united.

We need to keep it real, be courageous, and embrace the discomfort.

19

TEAM ELITE

I N 2024, Nick Saban retired from being the head football coach for the University of Alabama's Crimson Tide, a role that he had held since 2007. He is the winningest coach in the college's history and, in many respects, in American college team history. He's the two-time AP College Football Coach of the Year. He's won seven college football national championships. His career record as a college head coach is 292 wins, 71 losses, and 1 tie.

If you don't know football, trust me: that's an outstanding record.

There is a cult of appreciation around Saban that sets him apart from other coaches, but not for the usual reasons. His commitment to what he called the Process was unparalleled. The Process was his methodical and disciplined approach to building and sustaining not just a winning program but an *elite* program, composed of both principles and practices. His philosophy has garnered significant attention with speeches, books, and leadership case studies. Coach Saban excelled at creating this shared vision with everyone in the program, fostering a collective sense of purpose that drove an unwavering commitment level. He also held himself accountable to the same high standards he set for his coaches and players. He walked the talk, and everyone bought in.

In interviews, time and again, Saban has said that his goal is to create the psychological conditions in which players have a chance at winning. Interviewers ask him about his psychological skills with interest, because Saban doesn't manipulate to motivate. He believes that intrinsic motivation is the only way that his players will win. That means that Saban spends his time building players up from the inside out. Rather than making them feel as if they have insufficiencies and faults that have to be fixed, he gives them opportunities to step into bigger and better versions of themselves.

The culture that Saban has created in Alabama is one of accountability and inclusion. The Crimson Tide culture creates the opportunity for players to thrive, but ultimately success and personal growth are up to each person. At the same time, players are not the only people responsible for the team's ability to win games. The culture does not place players at the center of the organization. Everyone counts, everyone is an equal part of the University of Alabama sports community from administrators to fans. Together, there is a collective urgency to make incremental and lasting changes for the better. Every step forward is one that Saban's community takes together.

Saban is the last person who will take credit for his success. Pat McAfee, a sports commentator on ESPN, regularly says that when he tries to call Saban the GOAT of college football, Saban gets so uncomfortable that he deliberately changes the subject or walks away from the conversation.

Saban also tries to get one point across, a point that people sometimes miss.

Culture isn't just a buzzword. It isn't the "soft" side of anything. It's integral to how we get things done in groups. In sports or in business or at home, culture is all-encompassing, so much so that leadership becomes secondary to how the group operates.

So, in the game of football, when you hear "Roll Tide," your whole vibe goes right up. That's the highest bar you can set for a team. If you develop the right culture, it can sustain itself over many, many, many generations of team members, of new recruits, of leaders.

CLOSE TO the same time that Saban took over in Alabama, we moved to Florida. I would go on to live in Florida for the rest of my career, taking on several more roles of increased responsibility along the way.

I did have a hidden agenda though.

I wanted to be in Florida for Team Lewis. I wanted to raise my family in a place where the weather was favorable most of the year and we could build a life that supported our kids' interest in sports. Most importantly, we wanted to settle in one city for a while, one that was close enough to take a short flight to visit our extended families and one that allowed us to deeply connect with our community. Pepsi's regional HQ was in Orlando, so we were within a quick drive to Disney World. It was a dream come true.

Here's another thing about being in the South. They know football down here. If you live in the South, I don't need to tell you this, but for everyone else reading this, it's more than just a love for the game. Families breathe, drink, and eat football. At times, it can feel like there is almost no separation between a player and a fan. Yes, there's a lot of love for all sports, but even if you're driving down a dirt road in the smallest town, you're going to see the banners and the colors. Even if you're the odd one out and don't love football, you know what it *means*. You speak its language. Everywhere, people are watching and rooting for their favorite high school, college, or professional team. Even grassroots football is a thing here. And let's not forget that tailgating is taken very seriously, as it's a tried-and-true Southern tradition.

On every level, football is hypercompetitive. So is the beverage business. For me, my own process journey began when I took on the running of Pepsi's North America Field Sales Operations Organization, responsible for coaching all of Pepsi's general managers and sales leaders throughout the United States and Canada. I knew that coming down to the South required that I had to up Pepsi's game and I had to up my game. I thought to myself, "How can I invoke Saban to dial up my team's execution and performance?"

"We need to instill the Process into what we do each and every single day," I said to my team. "How we hire. How we train. How we sell. How we execute. How we lead. How we support one another. How we win. This is what it's all about."

I may have sounded a little more like a preacher than Saban himself. But the team knew where I was coming from. Everyone wanted to win. Winning meant more revenue, market share, profit, promotions, bonuses, and fun. It's not like it hadn't been done before. We needed to get back to our winning ways everywhere and every year.

One of the most memorable platforms that I created in the job was the Bottler Championship Series. It was a competition, a direct parallel to college football's Bowl Championship Series. Sixty US markets competed against each other using a set of common performance metrics. Results were published weekly, and I anchored a monthly webcast with regular local and regional cohosts and guests, just like a cable sports show. At the end of the year, top performers would compete in a playoff format, with others taking part in "bowl" games. The national champion and bowl winners were awarded team prizes and celebration moments like Super Bowl, NBA All-Star, NBA Finals, MLB All-Star, and NCAA Final Four tickets, as well as resort trips. We used our national sales meeting to celebrate the championship team with rings, jackets, and a huge North American celebration.

The program drove massive team excitement and healthy competition within the company. It didn't take much to feel the energy lift throughout the organization. Results were getting stronger, and local teams started to feel more confident. At the beginning, I knew that some of our team members were not all in on the idea, or not at all in. But I also knew that the Process was a winning approach to managing a team and managing their needs simultaneously. It's an approach that allowed all of us to build forward, a winning approach that I held in place for the next seven years.

TIMING, INDEED, is everything.

By 2018, we still were in our usual fierce battle with our primary competitor, but things were different. In the fall of 2017, the Coca-Cola Company reshaped its North America bottling system to operate as a fully refranchised system. The move was made to highlight the company's transformation to its new beverage partnership model. The thinking at Coca-Cola was this would unlock more consistency, coordination, and collaboration across the entire network and fuel local competitiveness.

Coca-Cola's move was significant. We knew the status quo wouldn't be enough.

Early in the morning one day in 2018, I got a call from my boss, Kirk Tanner, CEO of PepsiCo Beverages North America, to talk about the future competitive landscape. He thought that we needed to shift our thinking from "centralized decision-making" to becoming "nationally great and locally even better."

He had me at hello.

Our model, which was heavily centralized on a functional level, was working well for big-ticket scalable products and programs. But decisions about products destined for local markets usually took much longer to make. Just as Coca-Cola had done, we had to reorganize at Pepsi. Kirk was calling because my role was about to dramatically change. I was about to make a shift from national responsibility for field sales and operations to regional role as president of Pepsi's South Division.

It was time for a change. While I recognized my role in this new world of consumer beverages might be smaller, I also knew that my impact and influence on the business would be much larger than ever before.

Reorganizations can be amazing, but they also can be risky. For the rest of 2018, I had two roles. First, we had to end the current year as planned. Second, we had to get everything in place to launch the new structure and operating divisions by February 2019. Along with other key stakeholders, I was on the steering committee to bring Pepsi's new strategy to life.

I felt very blessed and fortunate to remain in Orlando and to take on this new role. I knew what was expected, and I knew what to do to get there.

"We are going to build and run a business that will be faster, stronger, and better than ever before," I said to my new team of one hundred senior VPs, VPs, and senior directors. "It's my mission to build the strongest team we have ever built."

This was my chance to build a championship-caliber team, my version of Nick Saban's Alabama. And that's what I did. I staffed all my key direct report roles with great leaders who were functionally strong and had solid performance track records. My executive team was very diverse. More than half of my direct reports were women; more than a third were from minority backgrounds. More than that, our skills complemented one another. Every gap in experience or capability was made up by several others. This holistic system included me. This team would win collectively, not individually.

For the first two weeks after the division launch, my new leadership team and I visited all thirteen markets together. We communicated our vision, our purpose, and our ways of working.

We wanted to be elite, so we named ourselves Team Elite.

It wasn't just a name. It was about our culture and who we were trying to be. Everything we did reflected our desire to become high performers year in and out. We wanted to have fun with it, so we branded our gear (Nike, Lululemon, Peter Millar, and more) with a new Team Elite logo. When we showed up at national meetings, we had fresh Team Elite looks on each day.

We were trying to make a statement, not to the rest of the organization but to ourselves. We had to really believe in Team Elite if it was going to happen. There are no days off when you are climbing up a culture ladder. I leveraged every teaching moment I could because I knew that I had to walk the talk. I was very hands-on. I wanted my leaders to see what I was doing so they could carry on cascading the same level of support throughout their teams. Word about Team Elite was buzzing. Associates throughout Pepsi expressed interest in joining our team.

At the end of day, we did it. Over the three-year period I was the head coach for Team Elite, the South led the company in performance on revenue, profit share, and human resource results. We were not only contributing significant value for our region but also for PepsiCo as a whole. We successfully led our people and business through the COVID-19 pandemic, as well as the racial inequity and economic challenges accompanying the strain of that era.

We were winners, winners at the highest levels.

As I left in 2022 to build the multicultural team, at least two of my direct reports were promoted into the C-suite.

My work on Team Elite was done.

IN BUSINESS, we care too much about who the leader is.

Leaders are not developing a business strategy by themselves. Yes, talent management is an essential part of driving a culture, because you have to have good players with the discipline to do the job well. When we're talking about football, we need players able to throw the ball or get out of a tackle. When we're looking at a business, we need our employees to be creative and get the job done. In either case, if we're actually interested in real success, everyone has to employ leadership skills.

Team Elite was competitive.

There's an old story that bears repeating. In crab fishing, the goal is always to end up with a bucket of fresh crabs for boiling and drenching in butter. The story goes that if you look down into that bucket, you'll notice that crabs will stop at nothing to fight their way out of that bucket, and that includes maiming and killing the other crabs around them if they have to. In a community, that crab bucket represents all of us trying to get out alive. The story teaches us that it's not worth it to bring someone down in order to pull yourself up.

And yet in competitive environments, we do tend to pull each other down as we try to get up. And sometimes in the workplace, we're made to feel that if we're not hypercompetitive, then we're going to lose out.

The culture trick isn't to be hypercompetitive against each other. It's to be competitive *with* each other, alongside each other.

Some leaders try to imply that a leadership role is something allotted to only a chosen few. That you have to be lucky to get in and up that ladder, and that luck isn't earned, it's innate. And sure, there is legitimate power in official leadership positions of authority. This includes the ability to set budgets, decide who to hire, set performance targets, provide or withhold rewards, and hold people accountable to plans. There's also expert power in the kind of leadership associated with being a subject matter or process expert, with or without an education behind that set of skills. Culture power is, on the flip side, about finding the real win—the recognition that everyone is a leader in their own job, by rights.

As Nick Saban shows us, humility can be a core leadership trait. This personal attribute manifests as a behavioral tendency to admit personal weakness, appreciate others' strengths, and take the time to learn from others. Teams with a high humility level can set the groundwork to decrease incivility and increase trust.

To get that group win, we have to cut out "crab bucket" behaviors entirely. No one was born with the God-given right to be at the top of that pile, and no one deserves to be stepped on for someone else to get to their pinnacle.

Leading Team Elite showed me and others that leadership works better when it's shared. In my experience, shared leadership is absolutely more profitable in both financial terms and in terms of employees' peace of mind. That's why it shouldn't matter whether or not you believe that workplace initiatives can truly create equity; the proof is the fact that when we're paying attention to equity, everyone wins financially, psychologically, and socially.

No matter how diverse the work group, all its members have one thing in common: the work. That means that efforts that celebrate a win or otherwise highlight the collective work itself will help raise the culture and raise each person up with it. When everyone wins together, we all win independently as well. Instead of starting with what each of us can do, we turn things around and start with all of us, all at once. We never have to separate the haves from the have-nots that way.

And isn't that what we really want?

20

GUARDIAN ANGELS

SHAQUILLE O'NEAL took his mother's last name, not his birth father's.

Shaq has said many times that his mother, Lucille, has always been his inspiration. Like Roland, Shaq's father, Joe Toney, struggled with drug addiction and was imprisoned for drug possession when O'Neal was a young child. When he got out, he didn't come back into O'Neal's life at all. Lucille set out to build a better foundation for her children. Toney's choice to relinquish his parental rights meant that Lucille's second husband, Philip "Sarge" Harrison, helped her raise Shaq. Even though the family moved a lot from the US to Europe and back again due to Sarge's US Army career, he was a reliable, sound father figure.

"Len Bias passed away from doing cocaine," O'Neal said in a 2021 interview about the former basketball star who lost his life in 1986 when Shaq was fourteen. Bias had been one of his heroes, as Shaq had shown promise in the sport as a six-foot-six teenager in New Jersey.

"My [step]father came in and tore me a new one. He came into the house and said, 'If you do coke, I'll kill you.' And I'm so young and dumb, I was like, 'I don't do Coke, I drink Pepsi.'"

Shaq credits Lucille and Sarge, as well as the Boys & Girls Clubs of America, for keeping him whole despite the fact that they struggled with a legacy of trauma, poverty, and addiction in their lives.

"You are tall. People are going to look up to you, so give them something to look up to you for," Lucille said to her son, teaching him the values of humility and community service.

When Shaq and I started working together the summer of 2019, I knew he was a great guy. I had watched him on the court. I knew that once he found his calling as a basketball phenomenon, Shaq had gone on to become one the greatest NBA players of all time, with four championships over nineteen seasons. I also knew that Shaq had been an ambassador, a marketer, and, even more than that, a catalyst for the Pepsi brand. He wasn't just a fan. He was and is an investor in Pepsi and a business strategist, roles that have evolved in parallel with his exceptional basketball career and eventually beyond it.

What I did not know before we met was that, more than anything else, Shaq had made it a priority to step up to Lucille's expectations.

What I did not know before we met was that those expectations would change the way that I saw my own responsibilities in the world and change them forever.

I HAD MOVED TO Orlando in 2008, and by 2019, it had become the longest I had lived in one place since childhood.

Sherene and I had built a real life for ourselves and for our kids. We had found our home base. Devon, Jordan, and Kellan were settled. It was a time for us to grow as a family and spend more time with each other, because I had locked things down at work and I didn't need to make the same kind of time commitments I had navigated a decade, two decades earlier.

Work was work. The business was still moving along at a rapid pace, and it was just at that moment that I had assumed the role of President of PepsiCo Beverages North America, South Division. Everybody was winning. The best group of executives with whom I've ever worked continued to be in charge. I had created a high-touch but disciplined human resource model that built ownership into who we were as a team and as individuals. We were not only making money for the company and for ourselves, we were feeling it. So far, so good.

I had grown under the umbrella of Pepsi, and Pepsi had grown under the Derek Lewis Effect. Pepsi and I were very much intertwined. The lines were very blurred.

But there was a point at which everything became more of the same. Same schedule, same routine, same game. I had done what I set out to do, and I kept doing it.

In the back of my mind, I knew that something had to give, but I couldn't quite put my finger on what I needed to do next. It was still a year before my world, the whole world, would shift historically as the result of the pandemic, and I was restless. I knew that the center could not hold, that the sameness would become entropy, and that would require me to redirect my energy to something new. I just didn't know what that would be.

When I first called on Shaq, it was all business.

We met, and we talked a lot about what it takes to get to the championship level. He was trying to frame up what that takes from a leadership standpoint, and I wanted him to speak at one of our Pepsi team events in Florida. It made sense. Shaq had developed a relationship with the brand, and he had represented Orlando and Miami for many years. We brought Shaq in to help our team develop a championship mindset, and it would have been a great cultural match if we had left things like that.

But at the end of that conversation, away from the corporate facade, Shaq and I spoke one-on-one.

Coming from similar backgrounds, we could see that there were some significant economic and social gaps in our community, issues that just weren't being touched. Both Lucille and my own mother had faced domestic abuse and addiction issues in the household, and both had worked hard to protect their children from the very worst possible outcomes of these social patterns. When you're wrapped up in a family system where drug use and mental health problems are par for the course, you don't really think about the everyday tenor of violence as abuse. You think about it as simply the way things are. It's normal because you don't know any different. I didn't know any different growing up in DC, and we didn't really talk about it at home, at school, anywhere. It just was what it was. A problem came up, we dodged, we deked. We got through that problem and the next one.

And let's get real. The person who bears the most in trying to manage abuse in the home is usually a mother. I'm not saying there aren't others who are up against the same violence, emotional or physical. But the statistics show that the struggle is more substantive and often more deadly for women, and especially for women with kids.

My mom was smart and lucky, and so was Shaq's, despite the fact that they both became mothers in their teens. They focused. They got through the pain of their family crises, and they did not give up.

Our moms had to set aside their own goals to make sure that we were stable. My mother didn't dare change jobs and try to get ahead because her federal government job was safe; it offered protections that other employment could not, and she had a real pension, a good one. It was reliable, and it made her reliable. So she didn't try to find another path; Mom just counted on her small wage increases year over year, and her safe mortgage. She got by. Lucille didn't go back to school to get her degrees until her children were well on their way to financially supporting themselves.

While a lot of our social support systems and values have changed over the last fifty-odd years, it's also true that nothing has changed. And not every family has the same ability and the same opportunities as Barbara Lewis and Lucille O'Neal.

For women and their children, survival has to come first.

THE HARBOR HOUSE of Central Florida provides an essential set of emergency services to women and their children in crisis, and even their family pets. It offers safe and unlisted shelter locations so that people facing violence in the home can get to a place where they are safe from being followed or attacked. Harbor House also provides a twenty-four-hour assistance hotline, counseling, legal advocacy, and justice for thousands of domestic violence survivors every year.

Supporting Harbor House was one of the first deals that Shaq and I planned together. I was privileged to sit down with Shaq's foundation and the Orlando Magic with the goal of creating a long-term partnership on grassroots initiatives that would help women.

Why? Because women and children are not protected enough, and they need to be. They need to be cherished. Their current social position has an impact on more than these women themselves. It's estimated that between two and ten million children in the United States witness domestic violence each year, in the same way that I watched my own mother endure abuse in the home. These children are at high risk for emotional, social, and behavior difficulties in life even if they themselves never face physical violence at home.

We developed Pepsi's Stronger Together program in partnership with the Shaquille O'Neal Foundation and the Orlando Magic in order to back social services like this one. We provided opportunities to uplift Black women that included internships, scholarships, mentoring, and entrepreneurial support via notable partnerships with *Essence* magazine, the Southwestern Athletic Conference, the Mary J. Blige Strength of a Woman Festival & Summit, the Women's National Basketball Players Association, and other HBCU activities. I was extremely proud to work with leaders of these organizations to collaborate on programming and activation.

But shelters and scholarships are not the answer to women's needs. Shelters in particular are last-minute, Band-Aid solutions. They don't get to the root of the problems that we're seeing in our families.

Every day, in every way, women need more support. They're just not getting enough of it from men, from companies, and from society. Women need men to give them the grace of taking a break, having a rest. They need a full family, a village, surrounding them. I'm talking to everyone here: if you are a woman, cis- or transgender, or identify as nonbinary, I want you to know that I see you. If you are a man, I know your lived experience, and I know we're not always getting the message that women are trying to share with us.

What I value so much in life, what my mom taught me, is that a strong work ethic and a high commitment to providing for children matter. She never wavered on working at night, for example, because she'd make a higher wage. I had to carry part of her burden: getting the younger kids dressed for school in the morning before she was up, and feeding them dinner when she went off to the night shift. She worked really hard. What I learned the most from her was the grind and that, as a parent, you take care of your responsibilities at work and at home, because providing for your kids is always going to be your number-one job. She appreciated that job because it allowed her to be the mom she wanted to be.

But at the same time, Mom didn't get a break. She didn't get time to become everything that she could have been because she became a mom when she was a teenager. The pathways that she could have followed, like college, like moving away from DC, were cut off. She had to take the opportunities right in front of her, and then she became the person she is today.

Roland could carry a conversation, he could make us smile, he had energy for days. He was the extrovert to Mom's introvert. But in not being there for her to lean on, in not giving her solace, in not cherishing her commitment to her family, they both lost out.

If we want to support women, then we have to create family cultures in which women are heard and seen and supported. Whether women are working as mothers or working as employees or entrepreneurs, it doesn't matter; women are working more hours in the day than men recognize. As families, we have to set expectations for supporting every family member.

You're not going to do everything right, but you can check in with yourself and each other. Do you feel good? Do you feel like your family is moving through a progression that you mapped out together? Are you liking what you see? If you were a child growing up in this family, would you thrive in this environment? What's your inspiration for the next five years of your life?

And here's the biggest question: Are you nurturing your partner in a way that makes sense *to them*?

It's not about the material goods, or whether you have the right job at the right time. That can and will arise if you have your values aligned with your goals.

It's about really listening when your partner answers those questions with you.

The good news is that once you hear those answers and pay attention, if things are not working, you are allowed to change things.

Change is something Shaq achieved, and it's something that I accomplished as well. Both of us decided that it was important to be an inspiration for the next generation of our families and to set the bar higher. It was critical to survive, and we needed to support the women in our lives and communities so that our family systems could advance.

WHEN SHAQ got drafted back in 1992, it was such a monumental occasion for the Orlando Magic franchise. That draft represented an open door for him, as well as a chance for him to pivot into becoming the man he is today.

When Shaq was up for the NBA draft, commissioner David Stern asked him a question.

"Stern says," as Shaq describes it, "even before the lottery, 'Do you want to play where it's hot or cold?' Now I don't want to create no conspiracy theory, but I told him, 'Definitely where it's hot.' Orlando was hot, and so was I. I didn't think nothing of it, and then at the draft he's coming up with the envelope and he's looking at the envelope and winks."

Eleven different teams had already printed up jerseys with Shaq's number on them. The Orlando Magic had a lucky roll of the dice, and Shaq got his wish.

I felt extremely lucky to be present in the room when Shaq's number 32 jersey was retired. It was good to see a lot of his old teammates and executives came back to mark the occasion. Shaq made 824 shots in four seasons with the Magic and was named an NBA All-Star every year he was there. In Orlando, he had 226 double-doubles in 295 regular-season games and 25 double-doubles in 26 playoff games, including Orlando's first NBA Finals. Even if you count up the numbers from every one of the six NBA teams he's played on, it's impossible to compute just how successful he's been. Shaq is among the best of the best. In fact, in October 2023, he was named Reebok's president of basketball.

I believe that the other side of Shaquille O'Neal is equally as important as his sport and business careers. He doesn't dress up like Santa, but his Shaq-a-Claus events deliver toys, clothing, food, bikes, gift cards, and even haircuts to children in need. There is nothing that his foundation won't consider giving. For over twenty-five years now, Shaq has been right there on the ground, connecting with kids, with parents, with communities to change the status quo.

When he took the stage at his jersey retirement, Shaq spoke with humility about his gratitude for his experience and for being part of the history of the team, cementing his Orlando legacy. Looking around at the crowd, I noticed the who's who of Orlando in the 1990s celebrating him as if it were a family reunion. In some ways, that was exactly what it was.

"You know, there's an old saying: never forget where you come from," Shaq said to us.

He may have been speaking about his first team, but I was remembering the words of tenderness and love that Shaq used to speak about his mother, Lucille. She was his original home, his first coach, and his biggest fan. She was his guardian angel, and he followed in her footsteps.

In Orlando, when you look up in the rafters at a Magic game, you'll always remember number 32.

I'll always remember the legacy of kindness that Lucille instilled in her son.

21

NOTHING LEFT ON THE TABLE

AT SIX-FOOT-NINE, Earvin "Magic" Johnson is a towering figure. I'm a tall guy, but I'm not that tall. And yet the moment I met him, I knew that I wasn't going to be looking up to him because of his height alone.

I was only twenty-three years old when I found out that Earvin, as he liked to be called, was coming to our new six-acre Pepsi facility. I didn't think I'd get to meet him that day because all of the department heads wanted to get one-on-ones with him, and his schedule was packed. Plus I was working all the way in the back office, deep in the warehouse and far away from the bustle in the managerial suites.

I knew he was on his way because everyone was talking about it. It was *all* anyone could talk about at Pepsi in 1990.

Less than two years earlier, Earl Graves had made the deal of his lifetime with Craig E. Weatherup, then President and CEO of Pepsi, to create the largest minority-controlled Pepsi-Cola franchise in the country. What Graves didn't realize was that Weatherup had even bigger plans for this partnership. It would involve bringing on board one of the most visible basketball players of his generation, still playing with the champion Los Angeles Lakers, to sweeten the deal. The $60 million agreement marked only the second time in twenty years that Pepsi had brought new ownership to its franchise network. Coincidentally, the only other Black-owned Pepsi franchise at the time was a Houghton, Michigan, enterprise owned by Dr. William Harvey, the president of Hampton University both before and after my education there.

What I didn't know that day was that Johnson was undertaking his due diligence for his partnership deal. He was looking into every nook and cranny in the facility, taking notes and talking to everyone.

All of a sudden, I heard the entry door to the hallway open.

My heart beating fast, somehow I knew that I was about to interact with one of the most famous people in the world.

In Johnson comes without knocking, wearing a pristine suit, looking really sharp. I jumped up.

"Welcome! Sit down, Mr. Johnson," I say, pointing to the chair across from my desk.

"What's going on, man?" he says with a big smile on his face. "You ready for the grand opening?"

I remember telling Johnson about who I was, what I did, and what I had done since I arrived at the company.

"I'm grateful to have you on the team," he said. "I look forward to having a tremendous experience here, as you know, as an entity here in the District of Columbia."

Graves and Johnson were a match made in heaven. Weatherup had given them a lot of runway and room to do what they felt necessary to build the business as an independent operation. That's why they were successful: Graves and Johnson had a lot of business acumen and a really high level of social capital in the Black community. It wasn't long before Johnson became a regular fixture at the facility. I got to take him out on the market tour on occasion, looking at Pepsi's placement in different parts of DC, explaining the intricacies of the business, how we worked at a granular level.

I was also there when Johnson made his announcement about having acquired HIV.

At the time, there was a lot of misinformation out there about HIV and AIDS, much of it stemming from the newness of the virus and the fact that getting infected was then very much a death sentence. It was also because of its perceived connection to the gay community.

Our world, just like Johnson's, got turned upside down.

The Pepsi team was, first and foremost, concerned about Johnson and his health and well-being, as well as the effect on his family. But there was also a lot of media attention to mitigate, a lot of new people knocking on our doors asking for statements. While we left the official responses to our PR team and Graves, behind the scenes we employees were worried on Johnson's behalf. Johnson wasn't just one of our owners; he was a sports hero and an all-round good guy. It was an emotional time for everyone.

All along, Johnson was in communication with us and was very reassuring, telling us through his words, his poise, and his confidence that everything was going to be fine. He showed a tremendous amount of class and grace under pressure.

He wasn't going to give up the fight.

He was going to fight hard for his health.

He was still going to represent his business and basketball interests, and he was still going to represent us.

Johnson reminded us to stand tall, stand strong, keep doing the work, and, above all, to keep making ourselves proud. That was his mantra.

I REMEMBER thinking at the time that we needed to be okay because Johnson was gonna be okay.

It was the first real business crisis I had to deal with, one that made me realize how important setting the tone for morale and providing emotional support are to my management skill set. Employees were distraught, and a lot of questions were coming in. Is he selling the business, do you know? Do you know how bad his health is? Did you know about this before he announced it? The questions were very heavy, and we didn't have all the answers. In fact, we didn't have *any* answers. The direction I received was to keep the team's focus on the business and the customers, so that's what I did.

But what Johnson did was even more impressive.

He quickly turned his positive HIV status into a positive for the community. Johnson became the spokesperson for raising awareness about the risk of HIV outside the gay community. At the time, heterosexual people weren't taking public health recommendations about HIV and AIDS seriously. Having a public figure like Johnson taking the lead shifted the conversation. It mattered that he didn't recede from the public eye and that he was honest about how he became infected. He talked openly about safe sex, getting tested, and the importance of sharing your HIV status. Johnson changed the game on our collective understanding of health.

It was a moment of clarity for me, watching Earvin Johnson take his HIV diagnosis in stride. He had every reason to give up, to cocoon the rest of his life away, and he didn't.

Whatever a normal person might do, he did the opposite. He kept working. He actually got back to playing basketball. He started the Magic Johnson Foundation. Johnson stepped up and used his voice to inspire people to be open, honest, respectful, and to own their futures. More than anything, Johnson saw this time as a transitional opportunity for him to understand what was important for him. He decided that his off-court life would be far greater than his basketball career, as great as it had been. He decided that his entire life was going to be (no pun intended) magical.

Johnson also stepped up and over obstacles in the community.

After the Rodney King riots broke out in Los Angeles in 1992, Magic said he was convinced that he needed to build his businesses in Black neighborhoods.

"When I think about Rodney King and the rioting, what I didn't like was that we tore up our own community," Johnson said in a recent Apple TV+ series on his work and life. "The Black community, we set our own businesses on fire, and that hurt South Central, Compton. That hurt so many communities."

Johnson's first project in the area was to build a movie theater, but to do that he had to create community partnership and decrease violence. He sat down with thirty-five gang members to make it happen.

"I said, 'I am not here to disrespect [anyone]. What I am here for is to say, this theater is going to help the entire Black community. I want you to come. I want your families to come. But you guys gotta agree that we can't have violence, outside or inside that theater. And I am creating jobs. So, if you guys got some guys who want to work, I will employ them.'"

More recently, he's expanded Earvin "Magic" Johnson Recreation Area to include 104 acres of sustainable and biodiverse land, a new community event center, and outdoor classrooms. He's now a part owner of the LA Dodgers and the Washington Commanders. He has built 125 Starbucks stores, compelling then-CEO Howard Schultz to expand the company's reach in urban centers and fronting half the money to do so. Magic improved an already successful business formula by knowing his customer better than anyone else and then overdelivering.

Because of what he's been able to accomplish, Johnson is a billionaire now. He's a wonderful businessman, I thought, when he first sat down with me in my tiny back office and listened to a twenty-three-year-old Derek educate him on things in our business, curious to learn what I had to say.

"You're helping a superstar!" I remember thinking. "But you're also being helped by an iconic business entrepreneur who's in your corner. I got Magic in my corner. I can't fail, right? I can't."

I had to take a page out of Johnson's book and look at my own life.

THE LESSON I learned from Earvin Johnson was that you cannot leave anything on the table.

It's an old business phrase, for those of you who haven't heard it before. Sometimes when you bid on a business project, you do so without knowing what your competitors are bidding. Everyone leaves a sealed envelope on the table. The goal is to present the lowest bid you can without losing money. If you bid much lower than your competitors without realizing it, you're basically giving money away.

In life, you don't want to leave anything on the table. You want to get everything you can out of the resources you have.

Earvin Johnson taught me that. Even when he was under the greatest health risk of his life, the greatest PR nightmare of his life, the greatest risk to his family stability, and the greatest risk to his wealth and security, Earvin Johnson left no crumbs.

Over the course of my career, I decided to do the same.

At every stage of the game, I made it a priority to add to, rather than subtract from, what was on my plate, based on what was important to me. I made it a priority to bring balance to my life so that no matter what was going on, I would not regret the choices I made and I would take advantage of every moment I had been given.

First and foremost, I was there for my kids in their best moments.

Even though I had a very hectic travel schedule, I made it to the majority of their games and was there to help them academically. It meant that I had to take a lot of late night and early morning flights, but sitting in that gym or embracing my child after they aced a test was priceless. I was there to witness some of the greatest moments my kids had in their academic and athletic careers.

I also chose to live in Florida.

For the last fifteen years and four roles of my career at Pepsi, I rigged the game so that I didn't have to move. I was able to do that because of my performance. But Sherene and I chose that not only so that we'd have a base for the kids, but also so that we'd get the lifestyle we all wanted to live. The weather is great, and the airport is easy to navigate. We live a short drive from Disney World, where we spend birthdays and special occasions. We're also able to benefit from access to sports throughout Central Florida, attending many events at the

Kia Center (formerly Amway Center) and Camping World Stadium.

As a resident of the community, I also contribute to charities and board service work.

I made a commitment to making my community better, both locally and with my continued involvement with Hampton University and Lake Highland Preparatory School, as well as the University of Alabama after my daughter, Jordan, pursued her two degrees and sports career there. I also serve on the Orlando Magic Youth Foundation and AdventHealth Foundation boards and scores of other nonprofits.

But I also have made sure that, no matter what, our family has fun.

My work at Pepsi transported me to thousands of sporting events over my career. I have been very blessed to attend major sporting championship events numerous times. I was actually doing work while simultaneously checking off bucket list items over and over again. But let's face it, sport is who I am.

Earvin Johnson didn't stop when his health almost took him down. I learned not to stop too. Even when my mental and physical resources were low, I knew that my attitude and my commitment had the power to make my kids better, make my family better, make my community better, make the schools I belong to better, make the boards I serve on better. And in turn, if I did make those parts of my life better, that process was going to make me a better person holistically.

I did it all. I do it all.

And I'm having the time of my life.

22

HISTORICALLY BETTER

"**M**Y PEOPLE WERE BROUGHT to America in chains," Dr. Martin Luther King Jr. said to the American Jewish Congress Convention in 1958. "Your people were driven here to escape the chains fashioned for them in Europe. Our unity is born of our common struggle for centuries, not only to rid ourselves of bondage, but to make oppression of any people by others an impossibility."

Dr. King wasn't just speaking about the everyday racism that many of us experience, especially those of us who were sidelined en masse by industrial genocide. He was referencing the historical connection between those who escaped the pogroms of Nazi Germany to find safety and solace at HBCUs.

In 1933, when the Nazi party took hold of the legislature in Germany, the Law for the Restoration of the Professional Civil Service was passed in order to prevent Jewish professionals from holding any positions in the government. Lawyers, doctors, and professors in particular had nowhere to work and nowhere to live that was safe. Thousands of Jewish scientists were suddenly forced to give up their university positions, and their names were removed from the rolls of institutions where they were employed, including already-famous scientists like Albert Einstein.

Many of these professional community leaders sought out assistance with relatives in the United States. While they had no problem immigrating to the US as refugees, antisemitism was loudly presenting itself in the halls of higher education even in the most progressive areas of this country.

And so in the 1930s, hundreds of Jewish scholars were hired at HBCUs. For the colleges themselves, it was an opportunity to expose their students to a different but aligned point of view and to gain access to some of the greatest minds in Europe. For the scholars, it was an opportunity to find a place of security in a time of crisis.

At Hampton, Dr. Viktor Lowenfeld, hired as a psychology professor, found refuge after escaping from Vienna as Germany began its occupation of Austria in 1938. He offered art classes in his spare time, and these classes elicited such enthusiastic responses that Lowenfeld eventually founded Hampton's art department.

One of the students Lowenfeld taught, and with whom he became close friends, was John Thomas Biggers.

"Viktor took us to the African museum and taught us the meaning of African art," Biggers later wrote. "He was also interested in our inner feelings, what made us tick. We express the most meaningful things in art."

In 1939, Biggers was sitting by his side when Lowenfeld received a letter from the State Department telling him that his entire family had been killed in the Holocaust.

"John, you are segregated," Lowenfeld said when Biggers offered his sincere condolences. "You have to ride on the back of the bus. You can't drink water in any building. You don't have toilet facilities. But they are not burning you en masse. They are burning these members of my family, and these people did not commit any crime. They were just born, that's all."

It was a relationship that placed fear into Biggers's heart that one day he and his own family might face a similar fate if he did not do something.

He had to do something.

In 1950, Biggers went undercover with his wife to investigate learning conditions at local Virginia schools. Posing as graduate students, they documented their findings of unequal education in a report for the NAACP.

The Biggers report was later used in the landmark 1954 case of *Brown v. Board of Education*. Their evidence resulted in the edict that struck down segregation in public schools.

Hampton was and is a place where people came together to fight racism and segregation, the status quo that keeps things difficult for those of us who don't have intergenerational power. The Emancipation Oak is not just a symbol: it continues to be a place of inspiration, identifying Hampton as not only a place of solace and safety from the outside world, but also of bravery and action and change.

HBCUs are not just historically Black; they are historically better.

"PEPSICO ANNOUNCES a new business unit dedicated to accelerating its efforts to address inequality inside and outside of our food and beverage companies. We have appointed 34-year company veteran Derek Lewis as President of PepsiCo's Multicultural Business and Equity Development Organization, with a $570 million budget," the February 18, 2022, press release read.

Since 2020, I had been balancing my time between my work as President of the South Division and the efforts I was making to galvanize people to support the Racial Equality Journey Action Committee.

We had scaled up our grassroots community service push quickly after George Floyd's murder in the protest summer of 2020. I was making calls to influence our suppliers and partners to come on this journey with us, and Pepsi Stronger Together expanded to include the Black Restaurant Accelerator, which supported Black-owned food service businesses, and Juntos Crecemos, for Hispanic-run small businesses. She Got Now became a multitiered program to support and honor young Black women attending HBCUs across the country. And we donated to the National Restaurant Association Educational Foundation to help struggling restaurants in partnership with the Florida Restaurant and Lodging Association and Shaquille O'Neal's "Shaq Bowl" restaurant challenge on Super Bowl Sunday.

But I demanded more of myself and more of Pepsi..

We had to move beyond the rhetorical version of DEI. We had to take action. I had to take action. I had not built myself up to this level, I had not become the man I made myself to be, to simply make money. I was good at making money. I had proved that and proved it again. But I had more inside me to accomplish.

Highest brand health scores across the company.

Highest retention.

Highest representation. My team's numbers of Black executive representation soared at nearly 25 percent, more than twice the company average.

Highest minority supplier spend increases across the entire company.

"What else? Are these numbers good to you?" I remember asking.

Everyone was laughing, nodding their heads.

"So here's what we want now. We need to set up a Racial Equality Journey Action Committee of at least twenty people at the VP or SVP level. This group will have the juice to galvanize executive cohorts from around the country to meet and execute a game plan to address this situation right now. Pepsi resources are going to change the course of the pandemic and do what we can for our Black and Hispanic communities, customers, and partners."

By June 2020, we had a strategy in place, with an almost half-billion-dollar commitment from our CEO, Ramon Laguarta, and an inform-engage-act framework to implement our ideas to increase Black representation at PepsiCo, support Black-owned businesses, and lift up Black communities over a five-year period.

Our ultimate goal was to increase organizational inclusion for all minorities and vulnerable people across the world. We created a plan to provide funding and grants and support to community-based organizations, to help educational efforts, to directly address homelessness, serve meals to people who needed help because of the pandemic. We created a plan to recruit a whole lot of new people. We also aimed to ensure that our own teams and the people in our communities were mentally strong, emotionally strong, while they were going through arguably the toughest challenge that collectively we've ever had. We moved resources immediately, and we made it happen through a cascading communication process in which everybody at Pepsi became aware of what we were doing.

A few months later, I was able to show my C-suite team that caring for our community meant big business as well.

"Well, racial equality efforts work. It's working. The investments are paying off," I said to the C-suite. "Because our customers and our community partners see that we're committed, and they see that what we're doing is authentic. And we're leaning in, and we're leaning in strongly. And we're all getting positive bounce-back because our consumers are rewarding our effort, through loyalty of consumption, through recognition, through support. You can see that your associates are happy and proud."

People nodded. People got it. I had done the right thing. We all had done the right thing, and we were continuing to do things right.

Under the surface of things, I reasoned at the time (and still do), was the fact that if the community wasn't safe and financially secure, then there was no way for a company to make more money out of that community over the long run. I had seen that from the very beginning back in DC. When the mom-and-pops made things work, we sold more overall. As a company selling a low-cost normal grocery-store good, Pepsi did better when the economy and its people were working in balance, in flow. So if we wanted to do better, we actually had to *do things better*.

The more we started having these conversations in the community, the more I knew we had to do better. We had to be a part of the solution. There were pressing issues in the community that we hadn't thought through, outside basic things like racism and gender roles and economic markers. The outreach I had been undertaking to get things right showed that there were so many factors that I hadn't considered that were having an effect on Black and Hispanic and other families' ability to thrive. The voice of the community told us that education, de-escalation training among police forces, homelessness, providing meals for those who were underserved, assistance for families who needed broader therapy support, medical and economic aid—all of these things really mattered to people.

One of my commitments was to give back to HBCUs at a level we had not accomplished before. We created a program called Historically Better. It was all about celebrating our culture on campus using homecoming weekends as the big activation catalyst, coming back together once a year and celebrating what HBCUs are all about. Yes, the program provided scholarships and links to Pepsi recruitment, but it also was an opportunity for Black joy. We wanted students to understand what exactly it was and is that makes our campuses historically better and to extend that feeling outward. We had food trucks come on campus and sell food, supporting Black small businesses, and we had a community element where we donated to local charities and programs to take the experience right down to children where they lived, inspiring them to get excited about their own future paths forward.

We had to pivot and become very agile across the board because we were addressing platforms that were unique and specific to each market. I made sure the team let go of any agenda. There wasn't one single push to get behind one charity, one cause, one community. In collaborating with our community organizations, we locked in on causes that were important to them, not just to Pepsi.

Taking such a transparent and open stance on connecting with communities made an impact with our employees. When our team members felt passionate about the commitment we were making to the cities they grew up in, they stayed with us.

Investing in our communities meant investing in long-term relationships in our teams. In the cities and towns where our employees and their families lived and worked, when they saw us show up there, that positively impacted how they showed up on the job as well.

Our aim was to leverage Pepsi's size, scale, and influence to positively impact social culture and diversity within and beyond our industry. By 2022, we had grown into a holistic, multicultural group, one not that different from a start-up organization designed to address inequalities for historically excluded people as one team.

LIKE I SAID, diversity is the one thing we all have in common. The fact that we each bring something unique to the table is a God-given blessing.

In business, diversity is needed more than ever. As the world changes around us, we need to stand up for issues that matter to people—that also includes brands and companies. We are not only responsible for reaching consumers; we are responsible for holding on to our employees and building trust in the workplace.

Numerous studies have shown that diverse teams out-perform non-diverse teams; it's not even close, it's by a wide margin. Diversity benefits companies across the board from faster problem-solving to increased profits to better decision-making. It also makes companies more innovative and creative because you have people with different perspectives and world-views bringing ideas to the table.

A diverse team is better able to understand and appeal to their company's customers, which is especially import-ant as our country becomes increasingly multicultural. At PepsiCo, our consumer base was very diverse, so it was important to have an executive team that reflected that and was well equipped to understand and engage with all kinds of consumers.

You can't be what you can't see, so having a diverse executive team is critical to provide women and minority employees with role models and mentors and show that it's possible for them to become leaders within the company. It also contributes to a more inclusive company culture and has been shown to improve employee retention and engagement.

We had an overarching plan on the equality journey, with specific pillars to go deep on. It was my job to ensure that we were doubling down on all those areas, to make sure we were exceeding the commitments that we put out into public awareness. It was also my job to hold myself to the highest standard of connection in our communities, and that meant diversity was taking the lead, not me.

It was my job to listen and learn and then, and only then, to commit and contribute, in that order. I used the stage that I had been given to tell a story of optimistic social change to my employees and, I hope, to the millions of people who would be affected by my actions.

We spent $400 million on helping our community.

We budgeted $570 million for social equity within Pepsi.

We made a business case for racial equality both inside and outside the company.

We raised the roof across every brand, every hiring practice, and every opportunity.

Historically better means being aware of not only the past but the ways in which we are contributing to the histories of our collective future.

None of us is alone in this world, and with our each and every chance to see each other clearly, well, those are gifts that we need to accept with grace. Our differences matter, but what matters more are the ways in which we galvanize each other to do the better thing, the best thing, for us all.

23

NOT THE STATISTIC

ACCORDING TO the American Cancer Society, the mortality rate for Black men who have colorectal cancers is almost 50 percent higher than for white men. Black men die more often than white men when they acquire the disease.

That figure is not based on the number of Black men who *get* cancer. Black men are only at a slightly higher risk of acquiring colorectal cancer and other cancers than white men. With some of the highest divides on that list of cancers, like lung cancer, there's a 15 percent difference between the treatment and outcomes experienced by Black and white men. But when you look at all cancers combined, the demographic differences are pretty much negligible, and in fact, Black women are less likely to get cancer than white women by about 8 percent.

Why is that?

On the surface, people might make a lot of assumptions, but the statistics just don't support those assumptions. If Black men were facing higher rates of cancer overall, you could talk about genetics, but the results of those analyses don't really bear out when factors like poverty come into play. You could talk about poverty and lack of access to insurance, which is very important to getting through a cancer diagnosis, but Black men survive many other cancers at similar rates to other Americans. You could look at lifestyle, but again if it was only a set of social and personal choices at work like diet and exercise routines or stress experiences, Black men would have much higher levels of cancer overall. In fact, if lifestyle was the governing factor, it would figure that Black women would likely have higher cancer rates as well, living with similar cultural norms in the same households and communities as Black men, and that just isn't the case.

All we know right now is that for Black men, colorectal cancer outcome differences are very, very acute in the United States.

So, when I was diagnosed with colon cancer, all bets were off.

IN MY NEW ROLE in Multicultural Business and Equity Development, I was traveling a lot. We had a lot to do quickly, and getting programs going across the US required me to stand up and make a lot of in-person appearances, especially as the pandemic restrictions were winding down in 2022.

I thought I had a pretty smooth travel routine, but little did I know that everything I was doing was taking a toll on my body and overall health. I felt as though I was in good shape and ate reasonably well, but I had passed fifty a few years back and assumed that the occasional digestive discomfort I felt owed a lot to the late night meals and business-dinner alcohol I had been relying upon to get by. I didn't really look at it like a systemic problem, and I used supplements to get by and provide relief. Sherene did not like that I did not get routine check-ups to stay on top of potential severe health issues. Instead, I always deferred to my once-a-year executive physical to check the box on my health.

"I'm good. I'm good," I said to her. We had excellent insurance and a great doctor. "They check everything. All the bloodwork, vision, hearing, they're doing stress test, motor skills. I don't think I need to worry."

Every year, I always received a pretty good report, scoring in the top quartile of patients in my age group. I did not get a report in 2022; I missed my annual exam due to scheduling conflicts.

The problem didn't really go away though, and it wasn't as if the signs weren't pointing me in the right direction. I was always getting those postcards from the doctor reminding me that I should get a routine colonoscopy because I was at the age now where I needed to be getting it checked regularly. I just never did it.

The signs from my body, I ignored those as well. I was used to grinding through everyday challenges.

But the blood in my stool meant I had to acknowledge that what I was experiencing was not normal. Even so, I tried to ignore it the first time or two. Honestly, I asked myself if I ate some watermelon. I chalked it up to hemorrhoids. But I also started to Google my symptoms before, finally, setting up a colonoscopy appointment.

I found out right away that there was a mass in my colon. While I was still groggy from the procedure, the doctor told Sherene that I had a tumor. But a tumor is just that; it can be a growth of any kind, benign or malignant. They don't really know if it's cancerous until they look at the cells they've biopsied under a microscope. In the meantime, the doctors put a tattoo on the mass so that it's easier to find when they eventually remove it.

"I got a tumor?" I said to Sherene when I heard the news. "So, what do we do with the tumor? How do we deal with the tumor?"

I didn't panic, but I was concerned. We validated that there was a real problem, and we knew that this issue was very much out of our expertise. But all we could do, on one level, was wait. There was more than a week between the test and the results. In some ways, it was a normal week, and in others, it was very odd. That very weekend I was being honored by the Hampton Alumni Association for outstanding alumni work, and I had to make an acceptance speech in NYC. After the Saturday night gala, Sherene and I came back the next day so that I could play in a charitable golf tournament on Monday morning that my pastor hosted in Orlando. While I was playing in the event, I got a call that I had been appointed to my first corporate board assignment. Momentum was good, really good.

But right after the tournament, I had to go home, shower, change, and head over to the doctor around noon with Sherene. My momentum totally changed direction.

"You have a cancerous tumor," he said. "And I need to refer you to a surgeon and oncologist ASAP."

"Right." I nodded.

"You know, it's a pretty sizable tumor. I checked to see if there were any signs that it was in your pancreas and I didn't necessarily see anything, but that needs to still be checked out further by your surgeon and by oncologists. Hopefully I'll see you next year."

It was a pretty cold meeting. As I sat there in shock, I still didn't know what the degree of severity was. Obviously, when you are facing cancer, you're looking for a high degree of specificity. Am I'm going to live? Do I have six months? Ten years? He didn't give us anything. He wasn't optimistic at any point in that conversation.

Sherene and I were looking at each other, confused. She and I didn't know what to do next. As we were walking out, we stopped to ask him some final questions.

"Do you have any recommendations on a surgeon or a college?"

"Yeah, there's one at the complex next door to us. Go check them out. Take these papers and let me know if they have any questions. Just tell them to call, but this paperwork should be a good start."

We walked to the office next door, but at three o'clock they were already closed for the day. We sat in the car, Googling oncologists for maybe five minutes. I could tell it was wearing her down. The high that we had been on over the last seventy-two hours was fading fast.

And then it just hit me.

"Calm down," I said to myself. "Pause for a moment. You've built a tremendous relationship network of people in your life personally, professionally. There's somebody that you should be able to call to give you some guidance on this."

"Why don't we call Brea?" I said to Sherene. "Brea went through cancer. She's a survivor now, and she would know exactly what to do."

I called our trusted friend on speakerphone.

"What's going on, Derek?"

"We're sitting there in the parking lot of the health office. I have a cancerous tumor."

"Okay, so first thing I want you guys to do is remain calm. You know why? We're gonna get on top of this. We got this. Do you have paperwork? I will call you back. So stay tight."

Within two hours, she had spoken to the chief medical officer in our health network and the top surgeon in the system.

"You're going to be under their care, and they're going to guide you through what needs to happen from here," she said.

Like clockwork, Dr. Victor Herrera and Dr. Mark Solomon called introducing themselves and proceeded to get me into a treatment plan right away.

"You're experiencing a lot of anxiety, a lot of stress right now," Dr. Solomon said. "But don't try to do anything differently and don't worry. I'm going to get you set up for CT scans. I don't want to provide an official prognosis for you yet, but from what I see I'm confident we can take care of this. I do hundreds of these procedures. And, Derek, I'm telling you: I think you're going to be fine."

The next week, I had planned a trip to Colorado for a golf and fishing trip. Dr. Solomon told me to go, but I had my scan two hours before I flew out. When I returned, he told me I had a localized tumor and that I would have robotic surgery in three weeks; only a small incision would be necessary to remove the growth. After that, they'd check my liver and lymph nodes just in case.

The next few weeks felt like the longest of my life. Every day, I was praying for a positive outcome. They only thing I felt like doing was playing a lot of golf. Every day was moving the needle closer and closer, but it felt like it was taking a long time. I was agonizing over every single day that passed. It was draining me because I couldn't control the strategy.

I don't think I had a good night's sleep before surgery day, but I popped up first thing in the morning ready to go. The prep work was challenging. The pre-surgery scrub, the eighteen hours of fasting. My body was ready. My mind was ready.

Devon and Kellan live in Orlando, but Jordan flew in the day before from Texas. She and Sherene checked me in.

"We're gonna start making him feel relaxed and comfortable," I remember the anesthesiologist saying to my family before the room went dark.

The surgery lasted nearly four hours. It was a long but very successful procedure.

"We'll make sure everything is tracking, and then hopefully we can get you out of here tomorrow," the surgeon told me when I woke up. "We took out twelve inches of your colon, but so far so good."

The doctors wanted me to get my body moving and my circulation going, so I was up and walking on their orders within twelve hours. My core muscles were extremely sensitive and sore, but I did what I was told. Within thirty-six hours, I was home, taking only 100 milligrams of Tylenol and a muscle relaxer for the pain.

Eight days after surgery, I had a wedding to go to in Atlanta. I couldn't drive, but I wanted to be there for my friends, and everything was taking place at the hotel. I needed to keep getting up and moving to balance the pain, but Sherene and I had a great time because we were celebrating a tremendous moment for our friends. And at the same time, I knew I was on my way to recovery and I felt much better.

MY CANCER STORY is not that of a rich man cutting the line. I was lucky enough to have health insurance, but I was on the same insurance plan as the rest of Pepsi's employees. My cancer story is, instead, about relationships.

I attribute my survival to two things.

The first is my relationship with the people around me. It's almost as if I've built a synaptic connection with people who have the ability to help lift me up, who will help me get by in times when I'm challenged. I am not a statistic because I had to make it a priority to build such strong connections to my communities at home and at work. My relationship with Sherene and my kids meant that I had a set of protections in place, people who looked out for me and were counting on me to survive. My relationships in our community meant that I knew people who had survived cancer and who could give me some good advice in a crisis.

The second reason I survived is because of my relationship with God. My faith is a personal one. As I look back, there have been moments when I don't know how I got out of difficult situations, situations like this one. I feel incredibly blessed. Knowing that, mere weeks before my surgery, I got some of the worst news I've ever received in my life and survived it. Every day, I felt that there was a lot of love coming in for me. I felt the vibe. I felt the angels. I felt people beside me, cheering me on and helping me endure what I was going through.

Memories flooded back into my consciousness right after my surgery. Back when I was about nine years old, I was flying down a DC alley on my bike and almost got hit by a car. Instead of a collision, I felt like I magically glided off the street right to the fence line. No harm, no foul. I didn't even fall down. Just like those times when I nearly got into car accidents only to catch myself at the last second; I should have gotten hit, and I didn't. Every time I've hit that edge, He's been there to get me out of it. I wasn't giving Him enough credit for it.

You don't have to believe in God. And I'm not some special person who's being gifted and saved and blessed over anyone else. But the fact is that I benefit from understanding that He is there for you and for me.

In 2022, I decided to retire. After my cancer journey, I knew that I did not have to grind my way through everything any longer. I knew I didn't have anything else to prove, and I also knew that I had a responsibility to move more fully into a life informed by service to humanity. It wasn't about giving back. I didn't just have a lifeline; I had a safety net. Through my lived experience, through my choices, and through my faith, I created a net so strong and so wide that I could do nothing else but hold it out to others. I knew that I had a chance to extend that net further out into the world around me.

It was fun being the Pepsi guy, but I'm not the Pepsi guy anymore. I don't miss being the Pepsi guy. I worked so hard for so long.

Now my mind is free. My schedule is clear of everything except the choices I make, the steps I take, and the service I offer.

My expectations of myself are higher than ever.

24

EYES ON THE PRIZE

HEN ALLEN MCKELLAR was awarded the keys to the city in Columbia, South Carolina, in 2008, I had just moved down to Florida. Maurice Cox, one of the most influential Black executives to ever work at Pepsi and my mentor, contacted me about attending this event. It was being held in one of my markets, and he thought we could really amplify things by showing up with several HQ leaders. It would also be my first time meeting Allen. Without hesitation, I committed to attend, and we began to plan it out.

It was a big celebratory night. All the local dignitaries were in attendance. The mayor, representatives from McKellar's undergraduate school, South Carolina State, and all of my local Pepsi team were there to give testimony about his success in school, in the military, and in corporate America. People made speeches about how he gave his support to up-and-coming Black leaders and individuals who wanted to contribute to society in a much bigger way. I invited Stephanie Capparell, who wrote the book *The Real Pepsi Challenge* about McKellar's experience and life, to join our group and fly down with us.

As McKellar and I sat at the dinner table together, we talked about how good he was at sales.

"I still have a job for you if you want to jump in, Allen," I said with a laugh to the eighty-eight-year-old man beside me. "I'll pay you well. I'll give you exactly what you need."

"I'm proud of you, you know." He smiled. "I can see that you're still advancing the cause. The company is still building off the momentum that we started back in the '40s."

McKellar was a legend, a hero. And sitting down with Capparell, I learned about all of the research she had completed to tell the story of Black people in corporate America. At the end of that night, I found that I was more committed than ever to making Pepsi a place of both opportunity and safety for people of color.

Every year after that, Maurice and I would take the time to visit McKellar at his home in St. Louis. We'd find a way to go up around his birthday, and we'd bring all of the local Pepsi folks together to go for lunch and celebrate him. In the ten years I got to know him before he passed away at the age of ninety-eight in 2018, he was full of spirit, his high energy infectious, his thinking laser fast. McKellar had known everyone back in the day. He told me about a meeting he had with President Dwight Eisenhower. As a matter of fact, he told me he'd met every living president during his lifetime. He also hung out with stars like Sammy Davis Jr. and other high-profile entertainers to help promote the Pepsi brand. He said what he wanted to say, and he still had a lot of swag, but back in the '40s, '50s, and '60s, McKellar truly was a pioneer.

Like him, I was meeting with influencers and hanging out with entertainers. Both of us were also still active in our churches and our colleges. The work that McKellar and his team accomplished as a Black sales group drove market shares that remained strong up until the present day. The commitment that we enjoyed from the Black community was because of the hard work of that team, and it was more work than I had ever really understood.

"A lot of my story is about the struggle," he said. "It was very difficult to go out on the road and visit Pepsi bottlers."

"Those luxurious Pullman train cars? I thought you rode in style."

"The look was important. I was dressed to represent with my suit on. Yet I was also asked to sit in the back of the trains. I couldn't get into certain hotels. I couldn't eat at certain restaurants. I had to meet my clients at the plants. It was always hard to do my job," he admitted.

"That does sound hard. Harder than I expected. You had the support of the company, but they couldn't help you when you were out in the field."

"With all the racial tension back then, people would call me, you know, choice words. I was on my own in that sense. I had to deal with it as it came. But I kept my eye on the prize, and I was very focused on delivering. And also I've loved being able to connect with the Black community everywhere I went on this map, and so it was worth every second. It was worth it."

It wasn't only McKellar who was challenging the social status quo. In the late '40s, Pepsi-Cola launched the influential advertising campaign "Leaders in Their Fields," a series of profiles spotlighting remarkable Black talent who were sending progressive shockwaves through their respective industries. The campaign featured the likes of United Nations diplomat Ralph Bunche and revered hat designer Mildred Blount. Later, in 1962, Harvey C. Russell Jr. went on to become the first Black officer appointed to a vice president position of a multinational US corporation, at Pepsi. To commemorate his watershed achievements, PepsiCo continues to honor associates' efforts in the fields of diversity, equity, and inclusion through the Harvey C. Russell Award, celebrated annually.

I had looked up to McKellar as a mirror to myself. The more time that I spent with him, the more I needed to engage with the reality of who I was and who I had become. On the day of his funeral, I stood up in front of his family and friends to speak about what his legacy meant to me and who I had become because of the sacrifices he had made. Standing on the dais at the church, I first read the letter that Indra Nooyi, our CEO at the time, had asked to be shared, and then I followed her words with my own personal reflections.

There is a long line of succession between McKellar and me, but he was the one who endured despite everything standing in his way. Sure, former Pepsi-Cola CEO Walter S. Mack was a trailblazer for the Black community when he hired the first all-Black sales team in 1940. That was a chance that Mack, among a lot of CEOs at the time, was unique in taking. But that sales team was a team of three people—McKellar, Herman T. Smith, and intern Jeanette Maund—among hundreds of white employees. And if Allen McKellar had not been as successful as he was, it's doubtful another Black sales team would have been hired.

McKellar himself had outlived a lot of his relatives. His youngest grandnieces and nephews surrounded me afterward asking questions. They didn't know much about his deep Pepsi connection and were overwhelmed and in awe of his legacy to Black culture, Black community, and Black corporate America. It was an honor to thank him and pay tribute to him on behalf of all the Black employees at the company.

WHEN I SAT in my hotel lobby drinking a glass of wine after McKellar's funeral, I thought hard about what it meant to advance.

At the time of my retirement, I was the highest-ranking Black executive at Pepsi of all time. I had clocked nearly thirty-five years on the job, I was fifty-six years old, and I was done. But in all the ways that count, I was just getting started.

As you are going through the game of life, you never know what the outcome will be. You do not know if you will live a long life like McKellar, or one that is cut short like my brother Butch. There are causes for longer or shorter lives, but sometimes it's just the luck of the draw.

When I think back on Butch's lived experience, we shared so many commonalities, so many factors that were exactly the same in our household growing up, that there is never going to be an easy answer as to why I survived and advanced and he did not. We were the same. We were brothers born of the same mother and the same father. And yet here I was, thirty-seven years older than Butch would ever be, alive and thriving.

With McKellar, the same could be true. He grew up under Jim Crow laws in the South, and many young Black men didn't make it through those horrific times. At the time of his birth, Hit the Coon and African Dodger were popular games at resorts, fairs, and festivals. Prizes were awarded for direct hits. Some operators gave the human targets protective wooden helmets covered with woolly hair, as the Jim Crow Museum tells us. In that same time, Black men were targets for fear-based lynchings that didn't ebb in any substantive way until the late 1960s. McKellar might have been a target just for having the wherewithal to get a decent job and ride in a train his own company was paying for.

Listen, as a community, we need to have real, authentic conversations about the root causes of continued racism. I strongly believe we need to keep it real, be courageous, and embrace the discomfort of facing realities head-on in order to make real progress on these issues.

In corporate America, we have the responsibility and opportunity to lead by example. If each company makes a commitment to fostering a diverse and inclusive workplace, with goals and measures of accountability built into its approaches, together, that's great.

But we also have to act.

We have to walk the talk.

We have to measure what we try to do and make changes every time we fall short.

As a country, we first need to recognize that racial inequality has always existed here, and that while much progress has been made, there is still much work left to be done. Real change can only occur when all of us recognize and commit to taking the tangible steps to effect that change. There needs to be education, partnership, willingness to lead, and openness to bringing others along with us on the journey.

But even more than this, each of us must trust in our own ability to find our own way to advance.

What McKellar taught me about myself and my own journey is that, like him, I kept my eyes on the prize. I realized, in looking back at his life and at my own, that we did not yield to fear of the unknown; we both embraced it. When an opportunity came up for me to open a new door, I said yes. The fact that I had to figure out what I was fighting on the other side of that door? That was a blessing, because the unknown unknowns kept me strategizing, and they also kept me connected to the people around me. I knew that I wasn't going it alone, and that my relationships meant everything to my ability to thrive.

Every day, I had made up my mind to do the smallest things, the things I could do over and over again, the things I knew would make each minute that much better for me and for others. I drew upon the skills I had to carry me through and advance by doing one thing at a time. Yes, I wanted to level up, but there was also patience in my impatience. I knew that all the preparation I had done throughout the years, all of the drills, the lessons I had learned, all those things can come to bear in a single moment every day.

BASED ON what I know, here and now, there are three keys to advancing in life, three keys that factor into delivering the life that you want.

These three words are big words. They feel like big responsibilities. But they are simple things. If you look at these words as answers rather than questions, then they become the easiest method forward over time. These words are reminders about what to maintain every day, what to check every day, what to live and breathe.

Results. Relationships. Reputation. These are the things that matter.

When I speak about results, I know that none of us is going to get it right every time. Instead, I'm thinking about those early sales numbers that I had to pore over every day on my first Pepsi route, right out of Hampton. It was always about the numbers: every day, every week, every month, my manager would be right there beside me, looking at where we were doing better, where we were doing worse. It was a lesson in transparency, not in building fear that I would fail. Knowing your results means that you have the power to change things. Looking at those results daily gives you every opportunity to shift the status quo. It's like when you avoid doing your taxes or ripping off a literal Band-Aid: it always feels worse than it is when you don't just do the thing right away. All of us need to be clear on where we have room to move the needle on our own dream goals, where we can hustle more at work, where we can step in and help our spouse or kids. Checking your results means asking questions and then taking the actions necessary to get things done differently, or patting yourself on the back for a job done well.

Motivational speaker Jim Rohn has said that the five people you spend the most time with will have the most significant impact on your choices and your character. But even more than that, I believe that your relationships are a key factor in your ability to advance. If it were not for my wife, Sherene, and our commitment to building Team Lewis, I would not have been able to get where I am today. If I did not spend time creating relationships with mom-and-pop groceries in DC and learning from their needs and wants, I would never have been able to build sales strategies that worked. If I didn't stress and reward collaboration and community within Team Elite, we would never have broken our sales records. Every place I moved in the United States, and every meeting I took, I remembered Earl Graves giving me those suits and thinking about the man I became because he trusted me, because I saw myself through his eyes. I have boundaries, but I am open to relationships and treating people like family, because giving trust gets trust.

Your reputation is your integrity. This is about making the right decisions, the ethical decisions, not the easy ones. In a world where a lot of people make choices based on how much money they can make without taking all stakeholders into account, you have to care about those stakeholders. Reputation is about building your capacity to make yourself known for being true to your word. Your word has to mean something. Why? Because your customers will remember. Your suppliers will remember. Your coworkers will remember. Your family, most of all, will remember. You want to be on the right side of history. Even if that history is a spreadsheet or a PowerPoint presentation or showing up with soup when your aunty is ill, you want to be remembered for what you brought into each situation to make it better, not worse. So when you ask yourself, "How am I showing up today?" are you showing up with words of respect and hope like Nick Saban? Or are you showing up and taking shortcuts that make our society that tiny bit harder to cope with? Having an impeccable reputation means that nothing will stand in your way of advancing.

Keep your eyes open and get the results you want.

Hold on to and nurture your relationships and count on your community.

Stay committed to your reputation and do the thing right.

25

DELIVER

I N MARTHA'S VINEYARD, Black families from across the
United States gather every summer to vacation, socialize,
and spend quality time with each other. It's common to
see multiple generations of Black families together at Oak
Bluffs, hanging out at Inkwell Beach, or eating delicious lob-
ster rolls at Nancy's.

The island has, in some ways, always been a symbol of
Black wealth, given its long history of welcoming communities of color who vacationed here. Because Massachusetts
was one of the first states to abolish the enslavement of Black
people, Martha's Vineyard was one of the safer places for free
Black families to both live and relax, and it still is. Now most
popularly known as a summer home to the Obamas and other
Black luminaries, in addition to people of all backgrounds, it is
a place of affluence, of community, and of long-standing peace.

As I end my work on this book, Sherene and I put the
finishing touches on our family vacation home in Martha's
Vineyard.

Our house there has a large green yard surrounded by verdant trees and flowers. It's only a few blocks down the road from Maria's home, Sherene's cousin. Her house is equally shaded by beautiful leafy trees in the hot summer months. Inside, our home away from home is open and welcoming. We chose a place with many large bedrooms so that our children, their partners, and our friends from across the country could come and stay comfortably.

The island is filled with beautiful golf courses. A short drive away, I can tee off any day of the week and enjoy drinks with my family, friends, and my Kappa Brothers.

But, best of all, when the parties have ended and everyone has left the island on the ferry or a plane back to Logan Airport, Martha's Vineyard is quiet.

It's a place I have created for myself. It's a place I want to be when I have a moment to myself. It's a place of solace.

For all the years that I worked and built my professional career, I deserve solace. Although my exciting post-Pepsi career has just begun (watch this space), it's me who is calling the shots now. I can ramp up my game in Florida, back home in the DMV, or here in Martha's Vineyard.

But no matter where I choose to be, I'm home.

FOR EVERY PERSON reading this book, I want you to believe you can be the person who delivers on your promise to yourself, just as I did.

Believe in yourself.

Believe in your network; believe in other people.

Take the time to breathe, to relax.

Don't stress yourself out.

I know you've been taught to take on the work, the world. For year after year after year, you've been grinding. You're always playing back the battle in your mind. You believe that if you don't do everything all at once, someone else will win.

Some of that's true. But not all of it. I have worked damn hard to get to where I am today, but I have not compromised my vision of the life I wanted to lead. I knew that I wanted to have a family, to cherish the time I had with them. I knew that I wanted to bring ease to my experience and take time out to enjoy Beyoncé's Renaissance World Tour and the Hampton Jazz Festival; to get courtside seats or field access at sporting events; to watch my daughter, Jordan, sign a professional basketball contract; to see my son Devon get engaged; to have Kellan follow in my footsteps to Hampton.

You can have drive and determination and also enjoy the game of life.

To get there, you can't quit. You can't stop seeing yourself as the lead actor in your own Hollywood movie. You can't drop the ball.

Everyone has a chance to be the person they want to be, and it might as well be you.

Show your tenacity.

Show your courage.

Show yourself that you will be the one who won't be defeated no matter what the odds. Be the one who is still fighting, still laughing, still crying, while you're still doing all of the things you need to do to succeed.

That's you playing the game you want to play.

CULTURE IS the foundation of excellence.

On one level, it was Pepsi's culture and its partnerships with people like Mariah Carey and Earl Graves that allowed me to leverage my skills and my determination into a long and successful career. But it was also Black culture that kept me moving forward and allowed me to be who I am. The support of my community allowed me to thrive, despite my family trauma and the challenges I overcame, and become who I am today.

Culture, wherever I found it, taught me how to grow and recognize what it means to be elite. That's why I learned to nurture corporate cultures based on values, not just based on the bottom line. Financial success, for Pepsi and for myself, has never come at the expense of equity because of the simple fact that supporting people means success. Excellence isn't only about being the best in business terms; it's also about community, commitment, and culture.

I never saw myself as an activist, but I did my work to raise the bar for the people around me. I made sure that I was committed to holding the door open for the next generation of leaders to walk through. And what's true for me is true for all people: leveling up means that we have to work together and that we won't settle for the bare minimum any longer.

We are the culture, and together we need to move from being go-getters to being go-givers.

We must see ourselves as capable of meeting our own elite expectations, namely the ones that we set for ourselves.

We must explore why the racial equality journey is not over, and strong cultures provide a foundation for the best kinds of changes for all of us.

We must believe in social goals that match financial goals, because without a strong community, we will not be able to build the capacity for social change.

We must witness our collective emergence from the past.

We must, and we will, lift each other up.

ACKNOWLEDGMENTS

I AM PROFOUNDLY GRATEFUL to the following individuals and institutions whose support and encouragement were invaluable in the creation of this book:

First and foremost, I would like to thank my entire family (Team Lewis) for their unwavering belief in me and their constant encouragement throughout this journey. I am especially grateful to my wife, Sherene, and my children, Devon, Jordan, and Kellan. Their love and support have been my anchor.

I also want to thank my mom, Barbara, and my brother Damon for being my biggest advocates since day one. I will always be indebted to them for their steadfast support. Thanks to my in-laws—father Wayne, mother Patricia, and sister Sherlon—who have offered tremendous support to us over the years, especially when we were far from home.

I am indebted to my friends, colleagues, and fraternity brothers who provided me with moral support, understanding, and high energy throughout this entire process. Your camaraderie has meant the world to me.

Special thanks to Elle Glencoe, whose expertise and guidance have been instrumental in shaping this manuscript. Your mentorship has been invaluable.

I am deeply appreciative of the publishing team at Page Two, whose dedication and expertise helped transform this manuscript into a polished book. Your professionalism and commitment to excellence have brought my vision to life.

Finally, I would like to express my appreciation to all those who supported me in ways seen and unseen. Your belief in this project has been a constant source of motivation.

Thank you all for being a part of this journey.

NOTES

Introduction

p. 1　*the Black population in the US had suffered:* César Caraballo et al., "Excess Mortality and Years of Potential Life Lost among the Black Population in the US, 1999–2020," *JAMA* 329, no. 19 (May 16, 2023): 1662–1670, doi.org/10.1001/jama.2023.7022.

1: Chocolate City

p. 16　*"What have the people of the District done:* Chris Myers Asch and George Derek Musgrove, *Chocolate City: A History of Race and Democracy in the Nation's Capital* (UNC Press Books, 2017).

2: Joaning

p. 22　*"'Jonin' is a quasi-ritualized game of verbal insult:* "Say Wha?" *Washington Post*, June 6, 1987, washingtonpost.com/archive/ lifestyle/magazine/1987/06/07/say-wha/09c557d4-2278-4065- 81ac-bc1b813532d3.

3: Haven

p. 35　*Forest Haven underwent a forced closure:* Murray Waas, "Bleak House," *Los Angeles Times*, April 3, 1994, latimes.com/archives/ la-xpm-1994-04-03-tm-41569-story.html.

4: The Real 007

p. 42　*3,446 lynchings of Black men accused of crimes in the South:* "History of Lynching in America," NAACP, naacp.org/ find-resources/history-explained/history-lynching-america.

p. 42   *Mary Peake, a free woman of color from the North, offered an education:* Lewis C. Lockwood, *Mary S. Peake: The Colored Teacher at Fortress Monroe* (American Tract Society, 1862). Available on Project Gutenberg at gutenberg.org/ebooks/ 20744.

p. 46   *I did not write this poem called "Pursuing the Dream":* This poem was handwritten by a member of the Kappa Alpha Psi line.

6: Pacesetting

p. 63   *Allen McKellar, born in 1920 in Abbeville:* Allen L. McKellar papers, 1942–1975 and undated (RL.11800), David M. Rubenstein Rare Book & Manuscript Library, Duke University, idn.duke.edu/ark:/87924/m17340.

7: Trust

p. 73   *As Chair and CEO of PepsiCo from 1986 to 1996, D. Wayne Calloway:* David A. Thomas and Stephanie J. Creary, "Meeting the Diversity Challenge at PepsiCo: The Steve Reinemund Era," Harvard Business School case study 9-410-024, August 17, 2009, hbs.edu/faculty/Pages/item.aspx?num=37751, 4.

10: Thirty Suits

p. 107   *"All of a sudden, Pepsi's market share became much more significant:* Thomas and Creary, "Meeting the Diversity Challenge at PepsiCo," 7.

11: Fast Exit

p. 118   *the homicide rate is highest among Black men:* Rebecca Wilson et al., "Surveillance for Violent Deaths—National Violent Death Reporting System, 42 States, the District of Columbia, and Puerto Rico, 2019," *Morbidity and Mortality Weekly Report Surveillance Summaries* 71, no. 6 (May 20, 2022): 1–40, doi.org/ 10.15585/mmwr.ss7106a1.

16: Hot

p. 158   *prefer the taste of Pepsi over Coke in blind taste tests:* George Van Doorn and Beyon Miloyan, "The Pepsi Paradox: A Review," *Food Quality and Preference* 65 (April 2018): 194–197, doi.org/ 10.1016/j.foodqual.2017.11.007.

18: Higher Up

p. 186   *states provided roughly 40 percent less for HBCUs:* Brian E.
Harper, "African American Access to Higher Education: The
Evolving Role of Historically Black Colleges and Universities,"
American Academic 3 (2019): 109–128, hdl.handle.net/10919/
86971.

p. 186   *students at HBCUs benefit more from the social support networks:*
Terrell R. Morton, "A Phenomenological and Ecological
Perspective on the Influence of Undergraduate Research
Experiences on Black Women's Persistence in STEM at an
HBCU," *Journal of Diversity in Higher Education* 14, no. 4
(2021): 530–543, doi.org/10.1037/dhe0000183; Gregory N.
Price and Angelino C.G. Viceisza, "What Can Historically
Black Colleges and Universities Teach about Improving
Higher Education Outcomes for Black Students?" *Journal
of Economic Perspectives* 37, no. 3 (Summer 2023): 213–232,
doi.org/10.1257/jep.37.3.213; Krystal L. Williams et al.,
"Meeting at the Margins: Culturally Affirming Practices at
HBCUs for Underserved Populations," *Higher Education*
84, no. 5 (November 2022): 1067–1087, doi.org/10.1007/
s10734-022-00816-w.

p. 190   *spending of Black households has increased 5 percent annually:*
Michael Chui et al., "A $300 Billion Opportunity: Serving
the Emerging Black American Consumer," *McKinsey
Quarterly*, August 6, 2021, mckinsey.com/featured-insights/
diversity-and-inclusion/a-300-billion-dollar-opportunity-
serving-the-emerging-black-american-consumer.

p. 190   *Black consumers' collective economic power is set to expand
dramatically:* Shelley Stewart III, "Marketing to the Multi-
faceted Black Consumer," McKinsey & Company, May 10,
2022, mckinsey.com/capabilities/growth-marketing-and-sales/
our-insights/marketing-to-the-multifaceted-black-consumer.

p. 191   *both markets represent a total of around a billion dollars:* McKinsey
& Company, "The Economic State of Latinos in the US:
Determined to Thrive," November 14, 2022, mckinsey.com/
featured-insights/diversity-and-inclusion/the-economic-state-
of-latinos-in-the-us-determined-to-thrive.

19: Team Elite

p. 201   *Teams with a high humility level can:* Chia-Yen Chiu, Jennifer
Marrone, and Michelle Tuckey, "How Do Humble People
Mitigate Group Incivility? An Examination of the Social Oil
Hypothesis of Collective Humility," *Journal of Occupational
Health Psychology* 26, no. 5 (October 2021): 361, doi.org/
10.1037/ocp0000244.

20: Guardian Angels

p. 204   *"My [step]father came in and tore me a new one:* As quoted in
Juan Paolo David, "'I Drink Pepsi'—Shaquille O'Neal Once
Had a Hilarious Response to a Life-Threatening Warning from
His Stepfather," *Sportskeeda*, April 21, 2023, sportskeeda.com/
basketball/news-i-drink-pepsi-shaquille-o-neal-hilarious-
response-life-threatening-warning-stepfather.

21: Nothing Left on the Table

p. 217   *"When I think about Rodney King and the rioting:* "Magic," *They
Call Me Magic*, season 1, episode 4, directed by Rick Famuyiwa,
featuring Magic Johnson, released April 22, 2022, on Apple
TV+.

22: Historically Better

p. 222   *hundreds of Jewish scholars were hired at HBCUs:* Gabrielle
Simon Edgcomb, *From Swastika to Jim Crow: Refugee Scholars
at Black Colleges* (Krieger Publishing Company, 1993).

p. 222   *"Viktor took us to the African museum: Beyond Swastika and Jim
Crow: Jewish Refugee Scholars at Black Colleges*, exhibition at
the Museum of Jewish Heritage, May 1, 2009, to February 21,
2010.

23: Not the Statistic

p. 231   *the mortality rate for Black men who have colorectal cancers:*
Farhad Islami et al., "American Cancer Society's Report on the
Status of Cancer Disparities in the United States, 2021," *CA:
A Cancer Journal for Clinicians* 72, no. 2 (March/April 2022):
112–143, doi.org/10.3322/caac.21703.

ABOUT THE AUTHOR

DEREK LEWIS is a strategic thought leader with extensive experience leading large-scale operations, driving sustainable growth, spearheading transformation, developing people, and inspiring change within communities. He's also a kid who grew up in Washington, DC, in the 1970s, protecting his younger brothers from hardship and abuse, and learning how to survive and advance in life.

Keep Advancing with Me

Through this memoir, I aim to impart crucial lessons on resilience, integrity, and the power of unwavering principles. I am here to offer guidance and support, inspired by my own experiences and challenges, to those seeking to lead impactful and authentic lives.

Invite Me to Speak

Onstage, I speak from my years of experience and success to inspire the next generation of leaders by intertwining my journey with a range of topics including leadership, business, entrepreneurship, politics, health, parenting, community, and culture, among others. To book me for a speaking engagement, please contact me via realdereklewis.com.

Tell Me What You Think

I'd love to hear what you've learned from reading *Survive and Advance*. If you think this book might inspire others, please drop me a positive review on your favorite retail site. It would really help spread the message.

Connect with Me Every Day

Give yourself permission to step right into a conversation with me. I'm open to hearing from you. Connect with me via:

◎ 𝕏 @realdereklewis   ⊕ realdereklewis.com
🇮🇳 linkedin.com/in/dereklewis1